THE SHORTEST HISTORY OF SCANDINAVIA

THE SHORTEST HISTORY OF SCANDINAVIA

14,000 Years from the Stone Age and the Vikings to the Happiest Nations in the World

MART KULDKEPP

THE EXPERIMENT
NEW YORK

THE SHORTEST HISTORY OF SCANDINAVIA: *14,000 Years from the Stone Age and the Vikings to the Happiest Nations in the World*

Pages 243–44 are a continuation of this copyright page.

Originally published in Australia by Black Inc. in 2025. First published in North America in revised form by The Experiment, LLC, in 2026.

The Experiment, LLC | 115 Broadway, 8th Floor | New York, NY 10006-1604
theexperimentpublishing.com

Library of Congress Cataloging-in-Publication Data

Names: Kuldkepp, Mart author
Title: The shortest history of Scandinavia : 14,000 years from the Stone Age and the Vikings to the happiest nations in the world / Mart Kuldkepp.
Description: New York : The Experiment, 2026. | Includes bibliographical references and index. | Summary: "From the Stone Age to "Scandimania," this book is a brisk, illuminating journey through 14,000 years of Nordic history"-- Provided by publisher.
Identifiers: LCCN 2025051308 (print) | LCCN 2025051309 (ebook) | ISBN 9798893030914 paperback | ISBN 9798893030921 ebook
Subjects: LCSH: Scandinavia--History | Scandinavia--Civilization
Classification: LCC DL46 .K85 2026 (print) | LCC DL46 (ebook)
LC record available at https://lccn.loc.gov/2025051308
LC ebook record available at https://lccn.loc.gov/2025051309

ISBN 979-8-89303-091-4
Ebook ISBN 979-8-89303-092-1

Cover design by Beth Bugler
Text design by Dennis Grauel

Manufactured in the United States of America

First printing January 2026
10 9 8 7 6 5 4 3 2

I would like to dedicate this book to Liisi,
who has supported me through every crunch time.

Contents

Preface

IF SOMEONE WERE ASKED TO NAME a positive attribute of Scandinavia, they would be spoiled for choice. The Nordics are world leaders in many fields: from social welfare, environmental protection, gender equality and conflict mediation to interior design, pop music, crime literature and cultural phenomena such as *hygge* and *sisu*. "Scandimania" has become a fixture of global culture, thanks, not least, to the Nordic countries' creative self-marketing, which has attracted attention and admiration around the world.

But not all Nordic history is unequivocally positive. In the High Middle Ages, Viking raids terrified much of Europe. In the early modern period, Sweden and Denmark were some of the most militaristic and expansionist states of their day, fighting many wars, both against each other and against other states. In the twentieth century, Scandinavia's neutrality was criticized as morally dubious. And while contemporary Scandinavian welfare states certainly ensure comfortable lives for their citizens, some say they stifle private initiative and encourage conformism. In recent decades, challenges have arisen from the politicization of immigration and the "return" of geopolitics to the Baltic Sea area, in the form of Russian aggression, especially toward Ukraine.

It goes without saying that any short history of a whole region must be very selective, in terms of what it covers and how it is structured. This book's narrative is partly chronological and partly thematic, with the latter aspect focusing on the broad question of Nordic successes and Nordic failures. These are judged against the aspirations of the Nordics themselves, as well as against the performance of their neighbors, both immediate and further away.

The Scandinavian success story—from the earliest human settlement to its world-leading status today—is not particularly difficult to tell. Perhaps that makes it especially important to also look at the ways the Nordics have failed or struggled. Some examples are an anthropogenic catastrophe in medieval Iceland, a eugenic sterilization program in Sweden and the tough compromises that Finland made during the Cold War.

Of course, my own interests and experiences also influenced the way this book turned out. Of the five Nordic countries—Denmark, Finland, Iceland, Norway and Sweden—I have spent the most time in Sweden and Iceland. The history of Finland, in my opinion, is the most interesting and varied. Denmark has probably the nicest capital, and Norway the most natural beauty. Yet I have tried to be as fair as I can to all of them.

Finally, I should say that I'm far from an expert on everything discussed in this book, and have very often relied on the research of others to inform and develop my understanding of Scandinavian history. To them I owe my greatest thanks.

1

WHAT IS SCANDINAVIA?

SCANDINAVIA, OR THE NORDIC REGION, comprises five separate nation states: Sweden, Denmark, Norway, Finland and Iceland. It also includes three autonomous territories. Of these, the Faroe Islands and Greenland belong to Denmark, and the Åland Islands belong to Finland. This book is, at least to some extent, about all of them.

It is worth noting here that not everybody agrees that the terms "Scandinavia" and "the Nordic region" (or *Norden* in the Scandinavian languages) can, or should, be used interchangeably. Very often, "Scandinavia" is used to refer only to Sweden, Denmark and Norway, while "the Nordic region" includes Finland and Iceland. But this distinction, whatever its merits, would make it difficult to write a history book. Finland was a part of the Kingdom of Sweden until 1809 and has always retained significant connections with its Scandinavian neighbors. Iceland gained full independence from Denmark only in 1944. It therefore stands to reason that they, too, should be included in any comprehensive Scandinavian history. In fact, the approximate historical territorial reach of the two ancient Scandinavian kingdoms—Sweden and Denmark—closely matches the boundaries of the Nordic region today. This is why, at least for me, "Scandinavian" and "Nordic" are best treated as near synonyms.

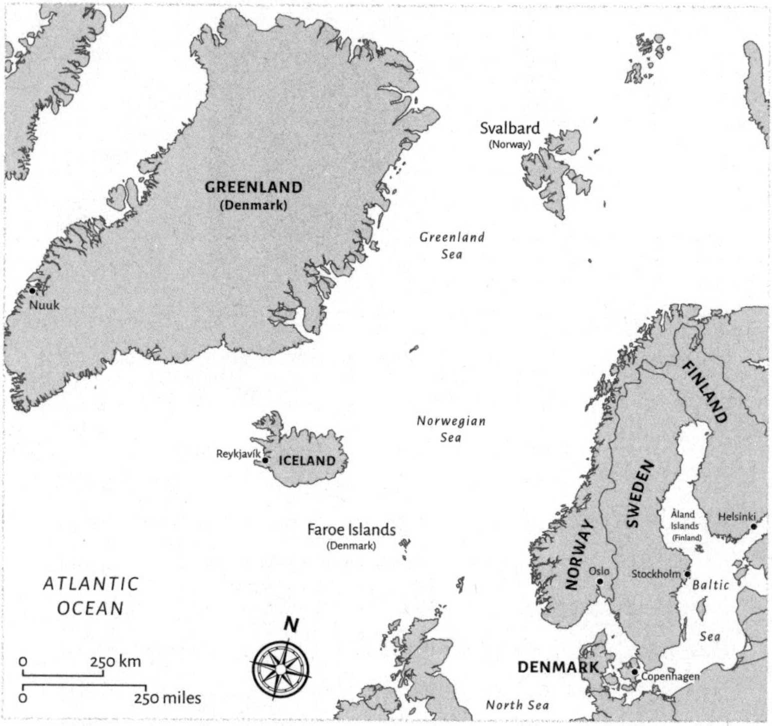

The Nordic region today.

While geographical and historical facts about the individual countries are important, they are not sufficient for understanding the region as a whole. A pan-Scandinavian history must pay particular attention to the developments and events that affected them all—often, but not always, in comparable ways—and how similar cultural outlooks and transnational connections across the region frequently steered them to respond to major challenges in a similar fashion.

Perceptions of the region are also important. It is probably fair to say that nearly every educated person has some opinion about Scandinavia. Most would focus on its differences from the European or Western mainstream, very often positive differences, casting Scandinavia as a sort of peripheral utopia, where the usual Western realities don't fully apply but are replaced by something marvelous—untouched nature, universal welfare, peacefulness. Admiration is implied, but also sadness that Scandinavian lessons are not easily transposed elsewhere.

The idea that the North is special is not new. In a way, it can be traced back to ancient Greek geographical writing about *ultima Thule*, a mythical place in Northern Europe "where the Sun goes to rest" (Geminus of Rhodes, circa first century BCE), and where there is "no longer any proper land nor sea nor air" but where these elements meld together, with "the consistency of a jellyfish" (Polybius, circa 140 BCE, citing Pytheas). Today, of course, instead of jellyfish, we talk about a special identity shared by the Nordic countries, and the various geographical and ideational features on which it is based. Yet there remains an inclination to compare Scandinavia with the rest of the West. As Danish historian Uffe Østergaard put it, *Norden* is "perceived as something non-European, non-Catholic, anti-Roman, anti-imperialist, non-colonial, peacefully inclined, small and social democratic."

Such ideas about Scandinavia do not entirely correspond to reality. The Nordics *are*, at least for the most part, obviously in Europe, there are clearly some Catholics living there, and counterarguments could be brought to claims about their social-democratic politics, peacefulness and non-colonialism. And with its total area of more than 1.3 million square miles (3.5 million square kilometers), the Nordic region can hardly be called small. Geographically, it is larger than the Republic of India [1.2 million square miles (3.3 million square kilometers)].

On the other hand, the population of Scandinavia is around 28 million—a far cry from India's 1.43 billion. It follows that Nordic countries are extremely sparsely populated, with an average density of only 20 people per square mile (seven to eight people per square kilometer). However, there is significant variation in density within the region, ranging from 8.8 people per square mile (3.4 people per square kilometer) in Iceland to 328 people per square mile (127 people per square kilometer) in Denmark proper. Scandinavia also has several large and fast-growing cities. The Stockholm metropolitan area alone has 2.4 million people—close to a quarter of Sweden's total population. The other Nordic capitals—Copenhagen (with 2.1 million people in the metropolitan area), Oslo (1.59 million), Helsinki (1.56 million) and Reykjavík (247,000)—likewise bring together a large share of their countries' populations. In this respect, Iceland is the most extreme case, with approximately two thirds of its tiny population of 366,000 living either in Reykjavík or just outside of it.

But what is perhaps the most significant perception about Scandinavia is one that Østergaard's list omits but nevertheless implies: namely that these five countries somehow belong together in the first place. What is it, then, that makes us think that they are all Nordic?

Most obviously they are situated close together. The Scandinavian Peninsula, surrounded by the Atlantic Ocean and the Baltic Sea on three sides, forms a natural point of gravity for any definition of the region. Since the peninsula is divided between Norway in the west and Sweden in the east, Norway and Sweden could therefore be said to be the most Nordic of the five Nordic countries. But Denmark, right to the south, is geographically very close. Finland, likewise, to the east of Sweden, sits right next to the peninsula. Yet there are outliers. Iceland and the Faroe Islands, situated far out there in the North Atlantic, are nowhere near the other Nordics. Greenland, moreover, is even further to the west—not even in Europe. Yet these three, too, belong together with the others. When defining the region, at least as important as geography are the Nordic countries' close linguistic, cultural, historical and political ties to each other. It is these that form the basis for the region's collective identity.

Culturally, it is very important that the mainland Scandinavian languages—Swedish, Norwegian and Danish—are mutually comprehensible. They have diverged in various ways from their common Nordic ancestor, spoken a millennium ago, but with a little bit of effort, a Norwegian can understand a Dane, and a Swede a Norwegian. The insular Scandinavian languages, Faroese and especially Icelandic, are more conservative and remain much closer to the original Viking language. This means that Faroese and Icelandic normally cannot be understood by mainland Scandinavian speakers who haven't studied them. But for historical and political reasons, most Icelanders and all Faroese also speak Danish, which gives them, too, unhindered access to the Nordic language community. Greenlanders are likewise bilingual in Greenlandic, which is an Eskimo-Aleut language, and Danish.

Similarly to Greenlandic, Finnish is not at all related to the other Nordic languages already mentioned, and in fact belongs to a completely different non-Indo-European language family: the Finno-Ugric languages, which also include Estonian and Hungarian. However, Finnish is also related to Sámi, which is one of the most significant minority languages of Norway and Sweden, and of Finland itself. Furthermore, in Finland a large national minority speak Swedish, the country's second official language, which means that all Finnish-speaking children also learn at least some Swedish. This means that it is theoretically possible for a Finn and a Greenlander to communicate with each other without resorting to English. The Nordic language community is a remarkable phenomenon.

Other cultural, historical and political commonalities between the different Nordics are too many to enumerate here. The following chapters of this book showcase many of them, from the Vikings to social democracy and beyond. But to bring this chapter to a close, it is worth emphasizing that, just like geography, culture and history alone cannot guarantee the development and maintenance of a regional identity. The people and the institutions in the region must also be invested in this identity on a deep, emotional level.

This investment can manifest itself in various ways. One important way is through regional organizations and institutions. These can coordinate on policy matters, encourage and fund pan-regional projects and fulfill other functions delegated to them by national-level parliaments and governments. In Scandinavia, such bodies include the Nordic Council, the Nordic Council of Ministers, the West Nordic Council and others, and occasionally they have played an important role in the region.

But institutions can only create a relatively "thin" regional identity—one that is superficial and reliant on concrete incentives, such as those created by funding. What makes the Nordics remarkable is their "thick" collective identity. This identity builds on a sense of natural, everyday affinity, and a willingness to favor their Nordic neighbors in many ways, as they would favor their own countrymen or other followers of their own religion. Indeed, "Nordicness" for Scandinavians is a kind of secondary order of nationhood, intermeshed with their primary one. It is impossible to be Swedish, Danish or Norwegian without being Nordic. Nordic is simply what they are.

2

PREHISTORICAL SCANDINAVIA

HUMAN HISTORY CAN BE BROADLY divided into two parts: the prehistorical and historical periods. What differentiates them is that the latter produced written records roughly contemporary with the events they describe. Such records allow historians and philologists to study the historical period in much more detail. The prehistorical period, however, is relatively silent for us. What we know of it comes almost entirely from archaeological data and whatever can be deduced from linguistic evidence such as place names, as well as from comparative and experimental studies.

It can be said that literacy and some form of written record-keeping arrived in Scandinavia with Christianity in the Middle Ages (eleventh–thirteen century CE). But this is not the full truth. The runic alphabet, or *futhark*, had been in use in Scandinavia since the beginning of the first millennium CE, with the earliest surviving inscriptions dated to about the second century. Very few examples of such inscriptions have been found, however. It seems that the use of runes became more widespread during the Viking Age (late eighth–mid-eleventh century CE). But even Viking-era inscriptions are typically short and laconic. Cut into wood or chiseled into stone, runes were not suitable for writing longer texts. Instead, almost all the historical, religious and legal knowledge needed by society was preserved in oral tradition—often in poetic form, to make it easier to remember.

The oldest form of the runic alphabet, or *futhark*.

Helpfully for historians, a relatively large number of foreign written sources about Scandinavia emerged during the Viking Age. This was a period when the region's relations with the rest of Europe and the world were rather intense, leading to better knowledge about Scandinavia abroad. With various caveats, we can therefore say that the historical period in Scandinavia began around 800 CE and that anything before that was prehistory.

The prehistorical period is further subdivided according to the prevalent raw material used to make tools and weapons at that time. In Scandinavia, these sub-periods were the Stone Age (up to 1750 BCE), the Bronze Age (1750–500 BCE) and the

Iron Age (500 BCE–800 CE). If one compares the duration of these periods to those in other parts of Europe, a kind of backwardness becomes evident. The Stone Age in Scandinavia lasted several centuries longer than elsewhere, as did the Bronze Age. Clearly, the region back then was not leading in technological progress and innovation. In fact, it is best described as peripheral.

The Stone Age cultures in Scandinavia were very similar to those elsewhere in Central and Northern Europe. The first known settlers who arrived in Scandinavia were nomads traveling together with reindeer herds. They came from the south around 14,000 years ago, following the ice sheet as it retreated after the end of the last Ice Age. The area that is now Denmark and southern Sweden quickly became the most important part of the region. It had the best climate and, due to its proximity to continental Europe, was the quickest to receive new cultural influences. As a rule, the earliest archaeological finds from all Scandinavian prehistorical periods come from that part of the Nordic world.

By around 4000 BCE, relatively stable communities of hunter-gatherers and herders had been established over a large part of the Scandinavian Peninsula. This was also the time of an important cultural transition from the earlier (Palaeolithic and Mesolithic) periods of the Stone Age to the later (Neolithic) period. Livestock farming and slash-and-burn agriculture, which already existed in the Near East around 10,000 BCE, now reached Scandinavia, but did not become predominant until around 3100 BCE, when it resulted in greater wealth and corresponding changes in social structure.

A clearer division of labor emerged between different social strata, and a rudimentary rural economy took shape.

Neolithic Scandinavia was a home for the Funnel Beaker, the Pitted Ware and the Battle Axe cultures, so named after their characteristic artifacts or styles of pottery. The Funnel Beakers, who had first adopted agriculture in Denmark and were known for building megalithic grave monuments (dolmens) on their collective graves, expanded in the fourth millennium to Sweden, up to the area of Uppland. Their advance was halted by nomadic tribes descended from the original Scandinavian hunter-gatherers, who became the Pitted Ware people. The Pitted Ware people did not adopt agriculture from the Funnel Beakers but co-existed with them until both cultures were overrun by the warlike and cattle-herding Battle Axe people toward the end of the third millennium.

The Battle Axe culture, using the battle axe as a status symbol, probably arrived from present-day Ukraine. Unlike the Funnel Beakers, the Battle Axe people preferred to bury their dead individually, making individual sacrifices. They also likely spoke a Proto-Germanic language. Since they were technologically more advanced than their predecessors, this language became the most dominant in Scandinavia. In hindsight, they therefore created the basis for future Nordic language unity.

The next big cultural shift was the Bronze Age. Although the first bronze objects found in Scandinavia date back to about 2300 BCE, the Bronze Age proper is considered to have begun around 1750 BCE, from when there is evidence of more extensive metal imports and metallurgical influences from Central and Southern Europe. Providing further evidence of close trade links are the many surviving Scandinavian rock carvings depicting ships and navigation. In addition to trading metal objects for amber and possibly other goods, Scandinavians were also smelting their own bronze. The regional culture of the period can be characterized as a fusion of the Pitted Ware and Battle Axe cultures.

Ships were one of the most common rock art symbols of the Scandinavian Bronze Age, reflecting the importance of maritime mobility during this time.

In the Bronze Age, Scandinavian influence also reached to the territories of present-day Finland and Estonia, where many Scandinavian artifacts have been found. During the fifteenth and fourteenth centuries BCE, in fact, southern Scandinavia became one of the centers of European bronze-working, with more Bronze Age swords having been recovered in Denmark than anywhere else. As indicated by the prevalence of weapons and helmets in Nordic burials, their society must have had a highly developed warrior ethos. It is also possible that it worshiped a mother goddess, who was later attested by first-century-CE Roman historian Tacitus, under the name Nerthus.

Toward the end of the Bronze Age, the climate in Northern Europe cooled, which led to an overall decline in trade and wealth and a corresponding simplification of the Scandinavian social structure, which had become quite hierarchical. This decline again helps to explain the region's essentially peripheral status compared to areas further to the south. Deeply affected by even small changes in climate, Scandinavia was only marginally habitable by standards of prehistorical agriculture.

The Iron Age in Scandinavia is considered to have begun in approximately 500 BCE, although the earliest iron finds date back a few hundred years earlier. The era is further subdivided into the Pre-Roman Iron Age or Celtic Iron Age (500–1 BCE), the Roman Iron Age (1–400 CE) and the Germanic Iron Age (400–800 CE).

During the late Bronze Age and the Celtic Iron Age, farming and cattle farming spread to the northernmost part of Scandinavia, as far north as Tromsø, in Norway, and the northern tip of the Gulf of Bothnia in Finland. In areas further to the north, hunting and gathering remained the main means of sourcing food. The spread of agriculture therefore intensified the contacts between the farmers to the south and the nomadic Sámi living in northern Scandinavia.

The Sámi people descended from Stone Age tribes around Lake Onega and Lake Ladoga, and they reached the Utsjoki

River in Finnish Lapland before 8100 BCE. At some point around 2000–2500 years ago, they adopted a Finnic language, which they still speak today. The Sámi hunted, fished, and herded reindeer, while the Scandinavian farmers had a culture like that of other Germanic settlements further to the south. By the early Iron Age, Scandinavia had thus become a zone of contact between two European cultures—the hunter-gatherers and herders of the northeast, and the agriculturalists of the south and west. Successively, the Sámi were pushed further northward by the newly arriving farmers.

European knowledge of Scandinavia continued to improve thanks to trade networks expanding northward during the Roman Iron Age. In Southern Europe, demand developed for goods from northern Scandinavia, which were in turn mediated southward by southern Scandinavian farmers. These were primarily luxury goods: furs, goose feathers, amber, slaves and even wigs made of blond hair, which were popular with dark-haired Roman women.

This high-prestige trade allowed southern Scandinavian rulers to accumulate wealth and further expand their influence, including in the nomadic northern regions. The runic alphabet, based on the Latin and Greek alphabets, was taken into use in this period and probably played a role in facilitating trade. In general, increased wealth, evidence of which has survived in funerary offerings, meant more openness to influences from Europe. The climate also became warmer during the Roman and Germanic Iron Ages, more arable land became available, and Scandinavia's population began to grow.

EARLY KNOWLEDGE OF SCANDINAVIA ABROAD

During the Iron Age, some knowledge of Scandinavia made it into ancient Greek and Roman written sources. The region appears on the great world map in Ptolemy's *Geographia* (circa 150 BCE), which includes four islands east of the Danish Jutland Peninsula, designated in Greek as Skandiai. The largest of them, Skandia, was probably not actually an island, as Ptolemy thought, but the region known as Scania (Skåne, in Swedish) in present-day southern Sweden. The other Skandiai were probably Danish islands.

The first known use of "Scandinavia" as a geographical term occurs in *Naturalis Historia* (78 CE) by the Roman author Pliny the Elder. The word may have originated from the Proto-Norse compound *Skaþin-aujo* (literally "dangerous island"), a reference, perhaps, to the perilous journey from the Atlantic to the Baltic Sea via the Danish straits of Kattegat and Skagerrak. Another work, *Germania* by Roman historian Tacitus, from around 100 CE, describes the life and customs of Scandinavians. It is therefore possible to say that Iron Age Scandinavia was already relatively widely known to be a part of Europe but in most ways still existed on the margins of the civilized world of the time.

In conjunction, these factors reopened the way for the greater hierarchization of Scandinavian society. In southern Scandinavia, private ownership of land and livestock replaced earlier communal forms of ownership, and some of the population became tenants. The earlier social structure, which Tacitus described as small groups of armed men (*comitatus*) led by a chief, now gave way to small, warlike chiefdoms that had close relations with the Roman Empire and later Europe's Germanic kingdoms. Their emergence was an important precursor for the Viking Age, as they allowed a single ruler to take control of many ships and warriors, and they led well-coordinated military campaigns.

The area that is now Denmark and southern Sweden continued to play an important intermediary role between Scandinavia and the rest of Europe, with the bulk of trade passing through its territory and waters. Over time, parts of the region further to the north in Sweden and Norway became politically and economically dependent on Danish rulers. Many rich tombs and the remains of impressive fortifications date from this period in Denmark and elsewhere in southern Scandinavia. For example, the fortress of Torsburgen on the Swedish island of Gotland is thought to have covered an area of about 0.4 square miles (1.2 square kilometers), which means that it must have been able to house an army of at least 500 to 1,000 warriors.

During the Germanic Iron Age, a Common Scandinavian (Ancient or Proto-Norse) language emerged, distinct from other Germanic languages spoken further to the south. It is attested in runic inscriptions, and by loanwords into neighboring languages such as Sámi, Finnish and Estonian. In the eighth century, it further evolved into Old Norse, the language of the Vikings.

3

THE VIKING AGE

THE TERM "VIKING AGE" BELONGS TO the Nordic historical tradition and is not used in European historiography more broadly. It lasted from the late eighth century to the mid-eleventh century, overlapping with the latter half of the European Early Middle Ages. Compared to the Germanic Iron Age that preceded it, it had a distinct character: that of an incredibly successful wave of Scandinavian expansionism to the rest of Europe (and beyond), by raiding, trading and settler colonialism. In Scandinavia, it was a transitional period between the prehistorical and historical times, ending with the region's integration into Western Christendom.

The etymology of the word "Viking" is uncertain, but it was not an ethnonym (a name for an ethnic group, tribe or people). Instead, it designated a profession or field of activity. Being a Viking meant being a seafarer and a warrior, something akin to a pirate. Elsewhere, the Vikings were also referred to as "Normans" ("men of the north") or "Varangians" ("men who took an oath"). The latter term was originally used for the Byzantine emperor's Scandinavian bodyguards, who had sworn an oath to protect their lord.

It is important to remember that seafarers made up only a small proportion of the total Scandinavian population. Most Scandinavians continued their traditional way of life as farmers and cattle herders. And even those who did undertake sea voyages did so in the summer, between planting and harvesting crops. Most of the time, the dreaded Vikings lived just like ordinary farmers.

The origins of the Viking Age present a complex puzzle, and any plausible explanation is based on a combination of factors. Firstly, it coincided with the first half of the so-called Medieval Warm Period (around 900–1300), when the climate in Europe and North America was relatively mild. This allowed for the cultivation of new lands, which resulted in population growth. In Scandinavia, this likely meant overcrowding and increased competition for scarce natural resources. Once the limits of agricultural expansion had been reached, the excess population had to find other things to do. One option, especially in coastal areas, was to earn wealth and prestige by trade and plunder abroad.

Thanks to the warmer climate, the North Sea and the Atlantic had relatively little drift ice, making them more navigable than before. Furthermore, Scandinavian shipbuilding and navigation had developed to a level that allowed the construction of exceptionally fast and robust vessels that could undertake very long voyages. At the same time, the increasingly close contact between Scandinavia and other parts of Europe had created a mutual demand for foreign luxury goods. Equipped with good ships, Scandinavians could now establish direct links with other regions and were no longer limited to mainly small-scale shipping through Denmark. It was probably through peaceful trade voyages, rather than raiding, that Scandinavians first became aware of the wealth of medieval Western Europe.

But the Vikings did not only voyage to the west. This was also a time when Arab slave-traders' dirhams began to make their way to Northern Europe, testifying to the wealth of the east. Swedish Vikings, in particular, traveled southward along the so-called eastern route, via the rivers of Ukraine and what is now Russia, to Constantinople and the Arab world. In absence of waterways between the rivers, ships were occasionally rolled overland on wooden logs. These expeditions were likely even more lucrative than those undertaken to Western Europe by Danish and Norwegian Vikings, but our knowledge about them is more limited, as very few written records survive.

One probable reason Viking voyages often turned violent was that while medieval Europe was growing richer and more stable, pagan Scandinavian traders likely found it increasingly hard to make deals with Christian merchants. This may have meant that the goods they desired had to be obtained by force. Furthermore, coastal raiding was a relatively safe activity. England, Ireland and Wales, for instance, were fragmented into petty kingdoms and were easy prey for foreign invaders. The beginning of the Viking Age also coincided with Charlemagne's wars against Saxon pagans, which meant that the most effective armies in Europe were deployed elsewhere.

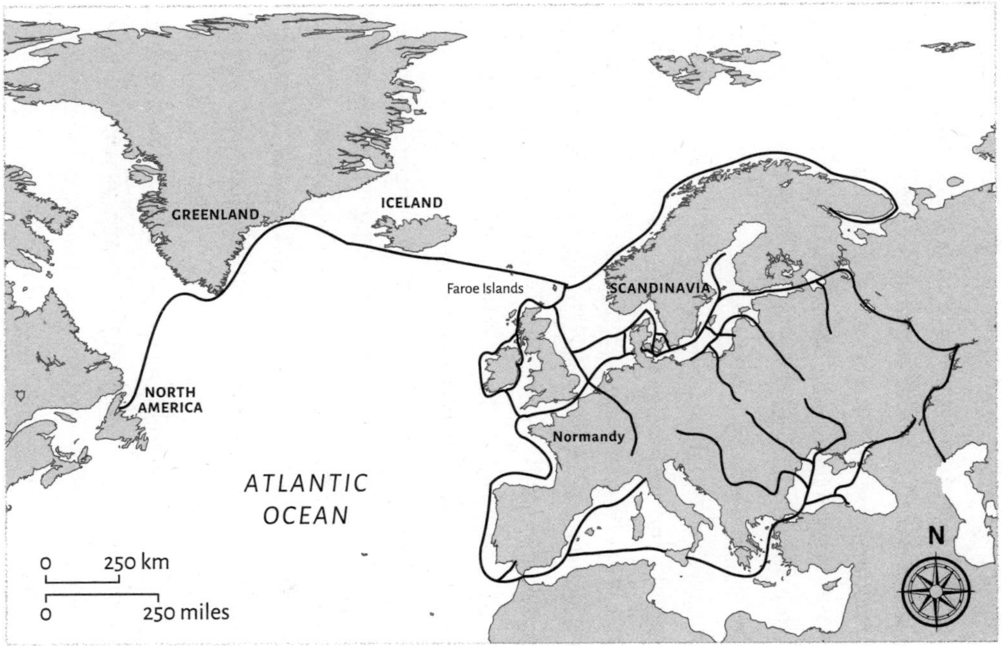

As this map of their various expeditions shows, the Vikings voyaged not just to Western Europe but throughout Southern and Eastern Europe and into the Middle East.

Finally, the Viking voyages had a lot to do with the early development of state capacity in Scandinavia, and the inevitable power struggles that resulted from it. Around the year 800, the first centralized kingdom in Scandinavia—Denmark—had begun to emerge. Similar consolidation of power into the hands of a progressively smaller number of rulers also happened elsewhere in the region. These new, relatively powerful overlords could, and possibly even had to, legitimize their rule by acquiring wealth and prestige abroad.

The stakes were high: according to the Germanic custom, the king was chosen by a general assembly (*þing*) of chieftains. What mattered at the assembly was the number of supporters, not the candidate's place in the royal lineage. This led to intense conflicts between different pretenders to the throne, who were usually descendants of the previous king. For them, amassing wealth and fame from overseas raiding expeditions could be a way of gathering support at home. Even those pretenders who were outnumbered and expelled from the country could still raise an army abroad and take the throne later—as did the Norwegian king Olaf Tryggvason (circa 964–1000) in 995—or conquer land somewhere else entirely.

Raiding and extortion overseas could also be an attractive proposition for kings already on the throne, as this was one of the few ways to fill the treasury in absence of an effective tax system. Most famously, the Danish king Sweyn Forkbeard (963–1014) managed to collect massive sums of so-called *Danegeld* in England by repeatedly extorting the local population. Not coincidentally, the Viking Age ended just around the time when political centralization in Scandinavia had reached a point where domestic collection of taxes had become possible.

The Viking voyages can be divided into two main types: trading and raiding expeditions, on the one hand, and attempts at settlement, on the other. However, the line between the two was often blurry; when settlement occurred, it was usually preceded by raiding in the same area.

The early Viking Age is best known for surprise attacks against poorly fortified coastal and island targets. Indeed, the beginning of the era is traditionally marked by one such attack, in 793, against a monastery on the island of Lindisfarne, just off the coast of Northumbria, England. This raid had already been preceded by one to the Isle of Portland, in Dorset, in 789, along with other similar expeditions. But Lindisfarne was important because it gave rise to the Vikings' international reputation as bloodthirsty raiders and conquerors. Before Lindisfarne, Scandinavians were apparently regarded as mostly peaceful merchants and not particularly feared.

The raid on Lindisfarne made it clear that pagan Norsemen had no reason to refrain from attacking monasteries and churches, which European chroniclers often saw as punishment from God himself. England was hit by an especially long series of attacks in the ninth and tenth centuries. Of the earlier Anglo-Saxon kingdoms, only Wessex managed to remain independent. Eventually, Wessex, too, had to start paying *Danegeld* to the Danes, and, for a couple of decades, the Danish king Cnut the Great (circa 990–1035) came to rule over the whole of England.

LAWS AND LEGAL TRADITIONS

Viking Age and medieval Nordic legal traditions were like those of their Germanic cousins, in that Nordic customary law lacked public law comparable to the Roman res publica. The only possible parties in a legal case were individuals or their kin, not society at large. Thus criminal justice was always personal, initiated by the victim of a crime or their representative.

Uniquely, Germanic law rarely employed the principle of talion ("eye for an eye") seen in many other ancient legal systems. Instead, offenses were resolved through *wergeld* (man-payment), a form of compensation paid to the victim or, in cases of murder, to the victim's family. This compensation varied, based on the crime's severity and the victim's social status. Another possible form of punishment was outlawry, which was applied if *wergeld* wasn't paid. The outlaw could be killed without consequence, forcing them to hide or flee. Finally, blood feuds between families did represent a form of talion, continuing until both sides reconciled or agreed on compensation.

Nordic laws were traditionally memorized and transmitted orally, until they came to be written down in the twelfth and thirteenth centuries, after the arrival of literacy and book-production techniques. The laws' codification stabilized justice by removing regional inconsistencies, and it bolstered central authority, as it allowed rulers, especially in Norway, to concentrate much of the judicial and legislative power into their own hands.

Around 795, Vikings also began raiding the coast of Ireland, where they established temporary strongholds for launching additional attacks. As Irish churches and monasteries were not as rich as those of the Franks and the English, the most valuable booty was slaves. The Vikings also became involved in local Irish power struggles. One of the greatest armed conflicts of the Viking Age, the Battle of Clontarf, in 1014, involved some 13,000 warriors, with Vikings fighting on both sides.

The early decades of the ninth century saw the start of the annual Viking sack of the Frankish coast, often taking advantage of conflicts between Frankish kings. Rouen was burnt in 841, and in 845 the sack of Paris was only averted when the huge sum of 7,000 pounds of silver was paid as ransom to the Vikings. In 857, however, the Vikings ended up conquering Paris anyway, which was easy, as the waterway along the Seine was free and the French coast unfortified.

Early on, the Vikings also began their attempts to settle, an activity known in Old Norse as *landnám* ("land-taking"). Partially, this was yet another way to solve Scandinavia's overpopulation problem, but it was also a useful strategy for defeated pretenders to the throne, who were often looking for land to establish their power base.

In 839, the Pictish kingdom in Northern Scotland was defeated by the Vikings and collapsed, and a permanent Viking settlement soon began to emerge on the islands of Shetland, Orkney and the Hebrides between Britain's northern tip and Norway. In the latter half of the ninth century, political opponents of the ambitious Norwegian king Harald Fairhair (circa 850–932) came to settle there, and in 875

Harald made the islands subject to Norwegian rule. Subsequently, many of his enemies migrated to Iceland. Having passed back and forth between Norwegian rule and Scottish rule, Orkney and Shetland officially remained Norwegian possessions until 1470–72.

Permanent Viking colonization of Ireland began in the 840s, and several modern Irish cities—such as Dublin, Cork and Limerick—originated as Viking trading posts along the coast (*longphort*, in Irish). Around 850, the first permanent Scandinavian colonies were also established in England, and soon covered a large part of the country. This Viking-dominated region, with York (*Jórvík*, in Old Norse) as its capital, came to be known as "Danelaw"—the area where the Danish law applied.

At least by the late 850s, the Slavic and Finno-Ugric tribes of the Russian region of Novgorod (Hólmgarðr, in Old Norse) were already paying taxes to Swedish Viking overlords. Eventually, there was an uprising against foreign rule, but this led to conflicts between the rebels themselves and political chaos. According to tradition, the Scandinavians were therefore recalled, and in 862 a Viking chieftain called Rurik (Hrærekr or Rørikr) became the ruler of Novgorod. In 882, Rurik's kinsman Oleg (Helgi, in Old Norse) founded the state of Kyivan Rus (Garðaríki or Svíþjóð hin mikla—"Great Sweden"), which controlled the trade routes between Scandinavia and Byzantium. Some Viking warriors also entered the service of the Byzantine emperor as bodyguards. By the end of the tenth century, however, Kyivan Rus and Novgorod had been culturally Slavicized, although it's possible some Old Norse was still spoken there up until the thirteenth century.

A similar pattern can be seen in other well-populated parts of Europe that experienced Viking settlement. In 911, a Danish or Norwegian Viking called Rollo (Hrólfr) was granted by Charles the Simple, the king of West Francia, a fiefdom of lands between the mouth of the Seine and Rouen, which came to be called Normandy, after the Normans. However, the Viking settlers were soon culturally and linguistically assimilated into the local population. The same also happened in England and Ireland, and eventually in the Scottish islands.

A different, and more successful, case of settlement was Iceland and the Faroe Islands, taken over by the Vikings in the 870s. These isolated lands were sparsely populated, if at all, and the Vikings therefore remained culturally and linguistically Norse. At the same time, the natural environment differed from what the settlers were accustomed to and was challenging to adapt to. Iceland went through a veritable anthropogenic catastrophe in the early centuries of Viking settlement, as its low-growing forests were cut or burned down, and the thin layer of soil that covered its volcanic rock became subject to major erosion. By the time the Norse colonists had settled on a sustainable way of producing food by fishing and sheep farming, much of the damage had already been done. The precariousness of Icelandic nature also contributed to a simplification of the social structure, with the result that Iceland became, rather uniquely in the Middle Ages, something akin to a republic of free farmers.

Early on, Iceland also became a starting point for further journeys westward. In 985, an Icelander called Erik the Red traveled to

Greenland, where two Norse settlements were subsequently established. They lasted until the end of the fifteenth century, when they died out due to climate change and competition for resources with the indigenous Inuit tribes. In the year 1000, Erik the Red's son Leif Eriksson further made his way from Greenland to North America, where he probably visited Baffin Island (which the saga writers called Helluland), Labrador (Markland) and northeastern Newfoundland (Vinland). This Viking discovery of America, described in medieval Icelandic sagas, was confirmed by archaeological discoveries in the 1960s, when traces of seven to eight Viking dwellings and a small forge were found at L'Anse aux Meadows, in Newfoundland. However, no permanent settlement was established.

The end point of the Viking Age in Europe is sometimes equated with the unsuccessful attempt by Norwegian king Harald Hardrada (circa 1015–66) to conquer England, which ended with his death in the Battle of Stamford Bridge against King Harold Godwinson of Wessex. But, more generally, Viking expeditions came to an end in the mid-eleventh century when royal power in Scandinavia had been sufficiently consolidated, and the Christian religion and church had gained a foothold in the region. From that point on, raiding became an obstacle to good trade relations with other countries, and sacking churches and monasteries became unacceptable for Christian kingdoms. Young Scandinavian nobles could henceforth satisfy their warlike instincts by crusading, and a rise in the social hierarchy was better achieved by entering the service of the king or the church.

In conclusion, it is fair to say that the Vikings were neither the first nor the only great seafarers. Nor were they always technologically innovative—they did not invent any new navigational techniques and were among the last to use sails. Instead, what was extraordinary was the geographical reach of their travels from Scandinavia through Russia to Byzantium and the Middle East, along the entire European coastline to Italy and North Africa, and across the Atlantic via Greenland to North America.

We also need to keep in mind that the Vikings were not only, or even primarily, significant because of their raiding and pillaging. They also played a more nuanced role as political and economic actors of their time, and even as cultural mediators. Their political influence could be particularly far-reaching. Viking activity paved the way for the unification of England and Scotland; in Ireland, the Vikings founded the first towns. They also contributed to the collapse of Charlemagne's empire, established the first states in Russia and Ukraine, and established the Duchy of Normandy, which went on to have a major impact on the histories of France, England and Italy. Because of the Vikings, Iceland, the Faroe Islands and Greenland were brought into the Nordic world. But at the same time, Europe's influence on Scandinavians in the Viking Age was at least as great as the Vikings' influence on Europe.

THE VIKING RAID ON LINDISFARNE

The Viking attack on Lindisfarne is famous because of an ominous entry in *The Anglo-Saxon Chronicle*, a collection of annals giving a year-to-year account of notable events in early medieval England. The entry for 793 CE notes:

> Here terrible portents came about over the land of Northumbria, and miserably frightened the people: these were immense flashes of lightning, and fiery dragons were seen flying in the air. A great famine immediately followed these signs; and a little after that in the same year on June 8, the raiding of heathen men miserably devastated God's church in Lindisfarne island by looting and slaughter.

For contemporary Europeans, the Lindisfarne raid was particularly shocking because of how rich and well known the monastery was. Lindisfarne had been an early center of Christianity in the Anglo-Saxon kingdom of Northumbria, and it was there the famous missionary St Cuthbert had served as a bishop and been buried after his death in 687. News of the raid, generally regarded as some form of holy vengeance, quickly reached the Frankish kingdom on the continent, and affirmed the seriousness of the threat posed by Viking incursions. In the years that followed, similar attacks quickly increased in frequency.

Coastal monasteries and settlements were particularly vulnerable to Viking activities. Their seaside location made them perfect targets, allowing the raiders to quickly escape by sea, carrying the loot with them. Improved fortifications and better military preparedness could have deterred the Vikings, but these measures were not easily achieved by the small and fragmented polities of the time.

4

THE RISE OF SCANDINAVIAN STATEHOOD

THE VIKING AGE AND THE FOLLOWING medieval period saw the establishment of the three old Scandinavian kingdoms: Denmark, Norway and Sweden. Two of them—Denmark and Sweden—have enjoyed nearly unbroken independence ever since, but modern Norway and Iceland, too, trace their statehood back to the Viking Age and the Middle Ages in various ways. Understanding these earlier times can therefore help us to understand the Scandinavian history that followed.

Behind the successful emergence of European-style kingdoms in Scandinavia was a long process of political consolidation that began in the Viking Age and to some extent even earlier. Eventually, it led to each Scandinavian kingdom being ruled by a single monarch, an outcome that hinged on the king's ability to accumulate enough wealth and influence to rise above his rivals. To a significant degree, this was facilitated by trade and raiding during the Viking Age, but even more crucial was Scandinavia's gradual integration into the sphere of Western Christendom. For ambitious rulers, working with the church was often the easiest way of concentrating power into their own hands.

In earlier times, Scandinavia had been divided into many small principalities headed by warlords and petty kings, with the ruler exercising his power primarily over people, not territory. The stability of a king's rule therefore depended directly on his ability to keep his subjects in line and loyal. But since the next king was elected at the assembly, dynastic continuity was weak and the likelihood of civil strife high. When there was no king—as in Iceland—the assembly (*Alþingi*) could even function independently as the only institution of government.

Over the course of the Viking Age and the Middle Ages, this would gradually change. The king's power over the people turned into power over territory, the revenue from raiding was replaced by taxes collected within the country, some rudimentary bureaucracy was established, and the judicial functions of the king and his entourage were expanded. Concurrently, the importance of the assemblies diminished, and they became either a means of exercising royal power (as in Norway and Denmark) or a rallying ground for the aristocratic opposition (as in Sweden).

All this was possible thanks to the expansion of Western Christendom into Scandinavia. At the time when the church was the only effective Europe-wide organization, it had an important role in facilitating the modernization of everything from relations between the states to the fundamental structure of societies. Wherever the church expanded, it brought with it medieval feudalism and kingship-based social order, as well as literacy, book production and knowledge of Latin. All these imports also brought a kind of medieval European normalcy and respectability to the emerging Scandinavian states.

For Scandinavia, which had remained pagan for a relatively long time, it was particularly important that Christianity arrived peacefully. It was not out of the question that the Nordic region could have become the target of crusades, as occurred in the thirteenth century on the close-by eastern shores of the Baltic Sea. Instead, Scandinavian rulers were able to convert themselves and their subjects mostly on their own terms. This ensured a strong degree of legal and political continuity with pre-Christian times, and especially with the nascent state-building process that had already begun in the Viking Age.

Finally, religious buildings were something that the new rulers directly benefited from, as priests were regarded as tenants of the owners of the land on which the churches stood. Much church-related income therefore flowed into the coffers of secular rulers. At the same time, it was the bishop's responsibility to consecrate churches and appoint priests, which gave the church an important lever to counteract royal greed. This meant an ever-present potential for conflict between the church and the state, so there were clear limits to their alliance, no matter how much they both benefited from it.

Scandinavian contact with Christianity had begun early, possibly even before the fall of the Roman Empire. However, it seems that baptisms of Scandinavians only became frequent from the ninth century onward. Viking chieftains who concluded treaties with Christian rulers, for instance, were often required to convert to Christianity, even if such conversions were not necessarily permanent. At the same time, the church gradually became a formidable political actor in Scandinavia itself, as various pretenders to the throne tried to garner its support and were baptized in the process. Some missionaries also made their way to the Nordic region, the most successful of them being one monk, Anskar (circa 801–65). His activities resulted in the first churches being built in Sweden and Denmark, and the allocation—if only formally—of the whole of Scandinavia under the Archdiocese of Bremen-Hamburg in Germany.

Until the mid-tenth century, most Scandinavian Christians were still baptized abroad, which only changed with the conversion of Scandinavian kings. In Denmark and Norway, this occurred in the tenth century, while Sweden remained mostly pagan for another hundred years. Just as the pace of political consolidation varied in different parts of Scandinavia, so did the spread of Christianity. But all in all, the first important milestones in Scandinavia's European transition had been reached by the end of the Viking Age—about year 1050. By that point, the three kingdoms of Denmark, Norway and Sweden had begun to resemble other contemporary European states in other ways as well. Further political consolidation continued, but its focus was no longer on the incorporation of new territory into the realm.

The first unified kingdom to emerge was Denmark, which was certainly best placed to do so as it was in the richest and most densely populated part of Scandinavia. Situated on islands and peninsulas, Denmark was easily accessible by waterways, which made its territory easier to control than that of Norway and Sweden, divided up as they were by thick forests and mountain ranges. Danish rulers also controlled the straits of Skagerrak and Kattegat, between the North Sea and the Baltic, which meant a stable source of customs income from merchant shipping passing through. Finally, Denmark was geographically closest to the wealthy countries of Western Europe, so it was nearly always the first to receive new cultural influences from abroad.

The earliest written references to the Danish king (*Rex Danorum*) date back to the sixth century. From the end of the eighth century onward, "Danish kings" are mentioned quite frequently in Viking Age Frankish sources, although it is possible that these kings were only ruling over Jutland. Nevertheless, archaeological evidence suggests that eighth-century Denmark must have already been a single state under a single ruler. Otherwise, it would be difficult to explain the existence of large-scale building projects such as the Danevirke fortress, in Jutland, and the Kanhave canal, on the island of Samsø. It also seems likely that the initial development of fast and reliable Scandinavian ships in the seventh and eighth centuries was driven by the need to move quickly between different parts of Denmark.

From the end of the ninth century to about 940, Danish statehood declined, but it then began to expand rapidly again under the Jelling dynasty, and especially its most famous ruler, Harald Bluetooth (circa 910–87). Harald, who was baptized in 965, proclaimed on a runestone of having "won for himself all of Denmark and Norway and made the Danes Christian."

FROM OLD NORSE PAGANISM TO CHRISTIANITY

When contrasting pre-Christian Scandinavian paganism with the European Christianity that arrived during the Viking Age and Middle Ages, it's essential to recognize that in many ways they were fundamentally distinct phenomena.

Perhaps the most significant difference lay in paganism's absence of a clear division between spiritual and secular realms. For a Christian, this distinction was marked, for instance, by the separation of the church—as both a place and institution—from their everyday life and its concerns. In paganism, no such difference existed. Legal, political and religious institutions were all deeply intertwined and associated with the same authoritative members of society.

In pagan thinking, it was positive human attributes—such as health or fortune, honor earned in travel and raids, political authority and judicial power, knowledge of myths and rituals, or skill in arts and crafts—that signaled the favor of various (good or bad) supernatural forces. Christianity, on the other hand, introduced the idea of a single transcendent authority—the creator of the world—with individuals such as priests and bishops acting more as learned intermediaries than divine protégés.

Where Christianity preached subjugation to the will of one omnipotent God, paganism knew of many gods and supernatural beings. Relationships between pagans and their gods were primarily transactional, based on sacrifices made and favors expected in return. The main sacrificial rites (*blót*, in Old Norse) took place in autumn and spring, and at the solstices. Major ritual sites included the likes of Lejre, in Denmark, and Gamla Uppsala, in Sweden: large settlements that likely had estates owned by nobles or kings. Such central places have primarily been found in southern Scandinavia, with some sites dating back to the fifth century.

Other sacred places were in natural transitional areas, such as shores and hilltops, but could also take the form of holy groves, springs and the like. Animals such as wolves, snakes, horses and wild boars were associated with supernatural forces and could hold significant religious roles. Certain foods and drinks, such as leek and beer, also carried religious significance. Old Norse gods and goddesses, which included Odin, Thor, Freyr, Freya and others, were likely associated with specific communities or families, rather than forming any well-established pantheon. Of course, there was also no pagan scripture, and myths were instead passed down through oral tradition, making them subject to change over time.

For pagans, conversion to Christianity thus represented a fundamental shift in world view, far greater than simply abandoning one faith for another. It is indeed likely that any understanding of Old Norse paganism as a religion in the narrower sense, as we see it described in some surviving medieval sources from the thirteenth and fourteenth centuries, emerged under the influence of Christianity. This is suggested, for example, by the adoption of Thor's hammer as a religious symbol in the late Viking Age, likely influenced by the Christian use of a similar symbol, the cross.

This is evidence of the extent of Harald's power, and likely his canniness in foreign policy, as paganism had by then clearly become an international liability. The claims of royal propaganda aside, Christian and pagan cultures initially coexisted in Denmark. Perhaps as a reaction to Christianization, the use of pagan symbols and funerals even increased initially. However, by about year 1000, pagan burials were no longer taking place, and, in personal amulets, the pagan Thor's hammer had been replaced by Christian crosses.

On this runestone—sometimes referred to as Denmark's birth certificate—King Harald Bluetooth proclaimed the unification and Christianization of Denmark, circa 980.

The next Danish king, Sweyn Forkbeard, was notable for his many expeditions to England but also for founding a church in Lund in about 990 as a challenge to the authority of the Archbishopric of Hamburg-Bremen. Conflicts with the archdiocese also continued during the time of Sweyn's successor, Cnut the Great, who visited Rome and started establishing permanent bishoprics in Denmark. It was during Cnut's reign that the extent of the Danish state reached its peak, incorporating England, Denmark and Norway. At the time, it must have seemed unlikely that separate Norwegian and maybe even Swedish kingdoms would exist at all. However, after Cnut the Great died, his empire quickly fell apart.

"Norway" had initially been a purely geographical term, denoting a trade route that ran northward along the Norwegian coast. However, tendencies toward political consolidation had become noticeable there during the reign of King Harald Fairhair (circa 850–932), who had managed to gain control over the coastal areas of Western Norway, important for trade with the north. Harald had also sent his son Haakon (circa 920–61) to England to be raised by King Athelstan. In Athelstan's court, Haakon converted to Christianity and later, as king, Haakon the Good brought English missionaries to Norway. Before his death, however, he reverted to paganism.

It was not until kings Olaf Tryggvason (circa 960–1000) and Olaf Haraldsson (995–1030) that Norwegian rulers managed to at least temporarily free the country from Danish overlordship and attempt to establish their own Christian kingdom. According to tradition, it was Olaf Tryggvason who Christianized the whole of Norway, including the hitherto pagan Trøndelag. Indirectly, he also brought Christianity to Iceland, where in absence of a king the people were converted by a decision of the general assembly around year 1000. Nevertheless, Danish supremacy in Norway was periodically restored, and it was only after Cnut the Great's death that

Norwegian kings were able to seize more permanent control. Eventually, most of medieval Norway was brought under Norwegian rule by kings Magnus the Good (1024–47) and his half-brother Harald Hardrada (1015–66).

In Norway, legislative centralization played an important role in political consolidation. By the tenth century, earlier local assemblies had developed into regional councils (*lögþing*, in Old Norse) with the authority to enact and change laws for a larger area consisting of several districts. Their emergence was linked to the growing authority of the king. By the eleventh century, the right to nominate assembly members had passed to nobles in royal service. Elsewhere in Scandinavia, the assemblies were not elevated to the same importance and remained institutions of local government. The exception was Iceland, which from 930 put in place a general assembly for the whole country, likely modeled on similar institutions in Norway.

In Sweden, the trend toward political consolidation was weaker, and Christianity took longer to gain a permanent foothold. This seems to have been due to the existence of an influential class of pagan chieftains, whose incomes depended on the flow of trade from the north to the east, and who were therefore less concerned with European pressures. Sweden's topography was also not conducive to centralized control of foreign trade, as was possible in Denmark and, to a lesser extent, in Norway. Furthermore, in Sweden, the king's main role seems to have been the maintenance of domestic stability, the success of which must have been predicated on a conciliatory approach to the nobles. If necessary, the latter could put up a powerful resistance to the king's policies, and the king had few levers to influence them, unlike elsewhere in Scandinavia.

Nevertheless, around year 1000, a king called Olof Skötkonung (circa 980–1022) is known to have ruled over both main parts of Sweden: Götaland and Svealand. Olof is also believed to have been Sweden's first Christian ruler, having possibly converted in 1008. Christianity seems to have been at first mainly confined to the province of Västergötland, where the first Swedish bishopric was founded around 990 in Skara. At the same time, pagan sacrificial rites continued in Uppsala until 1080.

It is only from the end of the twelfth century that evidence exists of a more permanent Swedish kingship recognized in both Götaland and Svealand. Nevertheless, the union between the two remained contentious, and medieval Sweden was certainly the least coherent of the three Scandinavian kingdoms. Instead, it is best described as a fragmented collection of districts, each with their own specific laws, taxation systems, units of measurement and so on.

Viking Age processes of political consolidation took place not only on the Scandinavian Peninsula but also in other areas inhabited by Scandinavians. The earls of Orkney and the Norse kings of Dublin and the Isle of Man also sought to extend their rule over larger areas. Even in Iceland, which started out as a sort of republic, power gradually accumulated in the hands of a small number of influential families. In the Icelandic case, however, this ultimately led not to the establishment of a separate kingdom but to the loss of its independence to Norway in the second half of the thirteenth century.

KING HARALD BLUETOOTH AND BLUETOOTH TECHNOLOGY

Harald Bluetooth Gormsson was the first major king of the Jelling dynasty, ruling over most of Jutland and Zealand, at least. Harald is famous for having recorded his claims to fame—bringing Christianity to Denmark and conquering all of Denmark and Norway—on two massive runestones that survive to the present day. He also constructed five large ring forts in strategic locations around his fortress, in what is now the part of Southern Jutland below Aarhus. These labor-intensive efforts at establishing actual and symbolic control over the country bear witness to Harald's likely unparalleled power in Scandinavia, as well as his understanding of the importance of propaganda. He is also responsible for the oldest known bridge in southern Scandinavia and is believed to have introduced the first national coinage in Denmark.

The origin of Harald's nickname is uncertain: it might have referred to an actual black tooth, as the words for blue and black were used mostly interchangeably in Old Norse. It might also have been a corruption of something else. In any case, it became world famous after 1997, when it was adopted as the name for the Bluetooth standard of short-range digital wireless communications. The relevance of Harald's nickname was later explained by how Bluetooth unites different devices, just as Harald united Denmark and Norway. Of course, in Harald's times, Denmark and Norway most likely remained united for only a short while, a somewhat unfavorable comment on the permanence of Bluetooth connections.

5

THE HIGH MIDDLE AGES: CENTRALIZATION AND EUROPEANIZATION

IT IS FAIR TO SAY THAT Scandinavia's transition from the Viking Age to the Middle Ages was a remarkably smooth one, facilitated by the wealth amassed on Viking voyages and a largely peaceful conversion to Christianity. Furthermore, the Medieval Warm Period continued beyond the Viking Age, ensuring sustained population growth. This made possible the easy emergence of the tenant system that became the economic base of the ruling elite.

After the church and the Scandinavian kings had jointly sidelined traditional pagan elites, their mutually beneficial alliance continued. The kings ensured the security of the church's possessions and income; in return, the church provided the state with educated advisers, international networks and a modern ideology of kingship. Soon after the end of the Viking Age, ceremonies such as coronation and anointment were introduced to reinforce the idea of royal status as something granted by God. The first coronation in Norway took place in 1163 or 1164, in Denmark in 1170 and in Sweden no later than 1210.

The church could also bolster the prestige of kingship through canonization of deceased rulers into sainthood. This was a useful way of giving their royal successors a role model to emulate, and everyone else a saint to venerate. The formal papal confirmation of King Olaf Haraldsson's sainthood in 1164 was particularly successful, with his cult spreading quickly in Norway and elsewhere in Northern Europe. Denmark's St Canute (circa 1042–86) had already been canonized in 1101, and Sweden's St Erik (circa 1120–60) was widely considered Sweden's patron saint, despite remaining formally uncanonized. However, neither of them managed to achieve the same popularity as St Olaf.

Thanks to its tax-exempt status and royal protection, the church successfully extended its social reach and influence. But there was also much potential for conflict in church–state relations. Right as Scandinavia was being Christianized in the eleventh to twelfth centuries, the church in Western Europe was undergoing substantial reform, aiming to free itself from secular control. From then on, churches and tithing were to be in the hands of the clergy alone, and only the clergy were to have the right to appoint other clergy, all under the unchallenged authority of the pope. In Scandinavia, just as elsewhere, these ambitions led to conflicts of interest, and sometimes open hostilities, between the church and the king. On top of that, the Scandinavian rulers' longstanding dispute with the

CITIES AND TRADE IN THE VIKING AGE AND MEDIEVAL ERA

Urbanization in Scandinavia began in the Viking Age; later than in some other parts of Northern Europe, such as England and Germany, where cities had been established centuries earlier. These early towns included Birka, in Sweden, and Ribe, Kaupang and Hedeby, in Denmark. Despite their small number and size, these early towns became hubs for trade and crafts, bringing together professional artisans and merchants, and featuring permanent marketplaces. Nevertheless, Scandinavia remained predominantly rural at the end of the Viking Age, with less than 10 percent of the population living in urban areas.

A second wave of urbanization began around year 1000 and saw the founding of towns such as Sigtuna, in Sweden, Århus, Roskilde and Lund, in Denmark, and Oslo and Trondheim, in Norway. The towns from the first urbanization wave largely declined, likely due to changing trade routes and geological factors such as land uplift, but possibly also because of their association with Viking Age paganism and royal power. Many of the newer towns, on the other hand, persisted into modern times.

Viking Age trade was primarily based on barter, often involving several steps of exchange. Toward the end of this period, silver became the accepted currency, and a form of monetary economy emerged. Since urban areas benefited from the more stable political and religious structures that now emerged, Scandinavian trade and commerce could expand further in the High Middle Ages.

Archdiocese of Hamburg-Bremen proved hard to solve.

The second important factor for medieval Scandinavian statehood was the European-style feudal relationships that now came to structure Scandinavian societies. Centered around landholding privileges that were granted by the kings to the nobles, feudalism created a privileged class of landed aristocracy with set obligations to royalty. These included the collection of taxes and local judicial functions, but also, and most importantly, military service, which in the Scandinavian case grew out of the so-called fleet duty (*leidang*, in Norwegian).

By the end of the Viking Age at the latest, and possibly much earlier, in all three kingdoms the king had acquired the right to levy a fleet for the purposes of either coastal defense or foreign excursions. When called up to *leidang*, all free men were obliged to provide ships, crews and equipment. The nucleus of the army remained the king's professional retinue, but conscription allowed for much larger forces to be called up. In Norway, *leidang* remained important for the defense and governance of the country until the early fourteenth century, as its topography favored maritime transport. The fleet was also necessary for communications with Norway's tributary lands in the west, notably Iceland and the Faroe Islands.

In Denmark and Sweden, however, the fleets were replaced in the thirteenth century by heavy cavalry and fortifications, following the example set by the rest of Europe. To fund this reform, Denmark and Sweden introduced regular taxes, which replaced the obligation to provide ships and crews. However, landowning nobles were exempted from tax, and were instead expected to enter royal service as horsemen (knights) when required. In Norway, too, a similar exemption from *leidang* was introduced to members of the royal retinue.

This meant that by the end of the thirteenth century, privileged, tax-exempt nobility had emerged in all three kingdoms, constituting a central component in the medieval societal structure of four estates: the clergy, the nobility, the burghers (townspeople) and the peasants. Together, the royalty, the church and the nobility formed a distinct upper class, the likes of which had never existed in Scandinavia before. At the same time, tax-paying farmers were relegated to a lower status, even if they remained personally free.

This new social structure also had a spatial dimension, with the churches and monasteries across the countryside representing the church, and the castles and fortresses functioning as focuses of noble power. At the same time, the king made the capital a more permanent center of his court and royal authority and was no longer required to frequently travel around, as in the Viking Age.

The relationship between royalty and nobility varied across the region. In Denmark and Sweden, where there was plenty of arable land and nobles were relatively rich, royal power was constrained by a strong aristocratic opposition. The Norwegian nobility was weaker and more dependent on the income and status associated with being in the king's service. This meant that a stronger royalty was in their own interests, and further centralization of power in Norway was therefore simpler to achieve.

Inevitably, however, the centralization of power proved contentious in all three kingdoms, leading to prolonged periods of domestic warfare. Monarchs would invariably attempt to make monarchy hereditary and to extend the king's legislative and judicial powers, but they encountered opposition from the nobles, who could, in response, extend their support to other pretenders to the throne. Eventually, winners emerged out of these challenges, enabling a further strengthening of the central government.

The relatively brief Danish wars of succession took place between 1130 and 1150, with the result that the strong Valdemar dynasty was enthroned, and Denmark once again became the leading state in Scandinavia. Norwegian succession conflicts lasted much longer, from about 1130 to 1240, and their centralizing effect was therefore even more significant, with the strong Sverre dynasty coming to power in the beginning of the thirteenth century. By 1163, Norway had adopted a new succession law making kingship hereditary, to prevent the possibility of co-regency and rivalry over the throne. This, indeed, greatly enhanced the political stability of the country, at least in the long run.

The Swedish wars of succession between the Sverker and Erik dynasties took place between 1130 and 1250. Having previously lagged in terms of state formation, Sweden caught up in the High Middle Ages. A separate Church of Sweden was established in 1164, and Sweden was finally unified permanently around 1250, under the Folkung dynasty. Largely, this was possible because the death of Danish king Valdemar II (1170–1241) had initiated a long period of turmoil in Denmark, fueled by bloody conflicts between the church and the state. As a result, the Danish dominance of regional politics was weakened, and Norway and Sweden benefited.

In every kingdom, the political and judicial institutions were affected by the royals' centralization efforts. Old-style regional and local assemblies gradually lost their legislative functions, and, with the spread of literacy, the kings were able to issue written decrees that were valid throughout the realm. Subsequently, the kings gradually acquired the power of veto over assembly decisions and, finally, the exclusive right to promulgate laws. This happened first in Denmark, in 1241, when King Valdemar II issued the new Jutland Law, and then in Sweden, when King Birger Magnusson (1280–1321) gave his assent to the Uppland Law in 1296.

In Norway, King Magnus the Law-Mender (1238–80) was able to go even further, and in 1274 successfully introduced the same law code for his whole kingdom, including Norway's North Atlantic tribute lands. This pushed Norway significantly ahead of the other Scandinavian kingdoms. Sweden first got a single law code in the mid-fourteenth century, and Denmark only in 1683. With some justification, Norway can therefore be considered the most modern Scandinavian kingdom of the high medieval period.

From the twelfth century onward, the Scandinavian kings occasionally organized larger councils of nobles and clergy from all over their respective countries, constituting, in a sense, nation-wide assemblies (*danehof*, in Danish; *riksmøter*, in Norwegian; *herredagar*, in Swedish). At the same time, in Western Europe, feudal councils were starting to evolve into representative assemblies, referred to as *parlamentum*, in which all four estates were represented. In Sweden and Denmark, however, the *danehof* and *herredagar* remained purely ruling-class-based, and could also present opposition to the king. In Norway, attempts were made to grant representation to the peasants, and the *riksmøter* were usually a lever for the church and the monarch against the nobility.

King Magnus the Law-Mender presents his national law to a lawman.

Perhaps due to the difficulty of organizing the meetings, these assemblies never became permanent political institutions. When, in the second half of the thirteenth century, the kings felt the need for more regular meetings of advisory bodies, new councils of state (*Riksrådet/Rigsrådet*) were formed in all three kingdoms, consisting of royal officials, the high aristocrats and the bishops. In the early decades of the fourteenth century, these finally became permanent institutions.

MEDIEVAL OLD NORSE ICELANDIC LITERATURE

The unparalleled flourishing of vernacular literature in high and late medieval Iceland certainly resulted in one of the most important Nordic contributions to world cultural history. Many questions remain about how and why these works were composed, and extant sources say little about their contemporary societal functions. But what we do know is that hundreds of medieval manuscripts have survived, containing texts in an astonishing variety of genres.

Icelandic culture after the beginning of settlement in the 870s was almost entirely oral, with works such as fairy tales, legends, eddic and skaldic poetry and even laws composed and transmitted without ever being written down. Literary culture arrived after year 1000, when the Icelandic general assembly took the decision to convert Iceland from paganism to Christianity. This decision stipulated, inter alia, that Iceland's pre-Christian elites—the richer and more prominent farmers—would retain their former privileges. In effect, this meant that Iceland's Christian priests and bishops would come from the same families as previous pagan priests and chieftains, ensuring a degree of continuity with pre-Christian traditions, and highly intertwined secular and ecclesiastical structures of power.

It is likely that this overlap of secular and clerical power had something to do with the development of Iceland's unique literary culture, which was characterized by writing in Old Norse, as well as Latin, and many texts with secular, not just religious, content. The first written laws, historical works and genealogies began to appear in the early twelfth century. Early on, Icelandic monasteries played crucial roles in manuscript production and the preservation of both religious and secular texts.

The contents of the earliest surviving Icelandic texts reflect a strong interest in local and regional history and genealogy. The prose sagas of the thirteenth century onward, including the kings' sagas and the sagas of Icelanders, likewise seem to represent the interest of the ruling families in their own past, relevant as it was to the bolstering of their political power in the present. From a literary perspective, the so-called sagas of Icelanders are particularly notable, coming in style and content closer to nineteenth-century realist novels than perhaps any other example of pre-Modern literary writing. Yet judging by surviving manuscript evidence, other genres such as romances were in fact much more popular in their own time. After Iceland came under Norwegian rule in the thirteenth century, many Icelandic manuscripts were also produced for export, with some surviving in Norway.

It was the advent of comparatively cheap paper in the fifteenth century that truly democratized access to books, leading to a broader spread of literacy across Icelandic society. *Sagnaskemmtun*, a popular form of evening entertainment that involved reading aloud from manuscripts, became widespread, ensuring that medieval texts continued to be preserved and copied.

Overall, Iceland's medieval literary culture reflected a unique interplay of local traditions, foreign influences and the integration of secular and clerical power, resulting in a rich literary heritage that to a remarkable extent still survives.

6

THE LATE MEDIEVAL CRISIS AND THE KALMAR UNION

THE VIKING AGE AND THE High Middle Ages marked a period of rapid political development for Scandinavia, which saw the emergence of European-style kingdoms and the gradual strengthening of the monarchy and church. In comparison, the Late Middle Ages was a time of prolonged crisis, not just in Scandinavia but in the whole of Europe. The fourteenth and fifteenth centuries were shaped by war, famines, epidemics, religious strife and peasant uprisings, all of which profoundly impacted European history. This crisis was a complex one, but can usefully be characterized as having had two main dimensions: a demographic-economic one and a religious-political one.

The demographic-economic dimension of the crisis was primarily caused by the end of the High Medieval Warm Period, which in the early fourteenth century gradually gave way to the "Little Ice Age." The cooling of the climate resulted in the stagnation of Europe's economy and population, and scarcity of food led to a fluctuation in grain prices, which affected domestic and international trade. Soon, measures such as bans on grain exports were introduced to stabilize cereal prices, which further exacerbated the threat of famine in the worst-affected areas. The resulting pressure on landowners to raise productivity while keeping wages low led to large-scale farm depopulation and frequent peasant uprisings. Poorly armed peasants were nearly always defeated, but the threat of insurrection significantly strained relations between the nobility and the peasantry.

A grim solution to the problem of overpopulation was provided by the Great Famine of 1315–17 and the Black Death pandemic of circa 1346–53, which, respectively, led to the death of 10 percent and 30–50 percent of Europe's population. As the falling agricultural yields could no longer sustain the same number of people, immune systems weakened by malnutrition presented ideal conditions for the spread of diseases such as the plague.

To this day, the Black Death remains one of the most devastating pandemics in European history, from which it took around 150 years for Europe's population to recover. Of course, bubonic plague had occurred before and continued to break out, to an extent, until well into the eighteenth century. What made the Black Death different was its rapid spread and rate of fatality. It reached Italy in early 1348; England in June 1348; Germany, Sweden and Denmark in 1348–50; Norway in 1349; Russia in 1351; Iceland in 1349. Depopulation once again had an impact on the economy and social relations, with the sudden surplus of fertile land and shortage of labor contributing to the emergence of serfdom in some areas of Europe, and the improvement of peasant rights in others.

A central factor of the religious-political dimension of the crisis was the schism in the Catholic Church from 1378 to 1417, with two rival popes, one in Rome and one in Avignon, each claiming authority over the other. The addition of a third pope in Pisa, from 1409 to 1410, further diminished the prestige of the papacy. The loss of trust in the church intersected with other contemporary misfortunes, and the church was suspected of having failed to prevent God's wrath, or even having caused it. Popular discontent with the church grew among the faithful, who accused clergy of being low in education, having secular interests and neglecting their duties. Alternative forms of religiosity that advocated for a return to biblical and apostolic models gained popularity.

Additionally, the Hundred Years' War, between England and France (1337–1453), introduced important innovations in warfare, such as widespread use of gunpowder and the first permanent armies. Slowly but surely, the era of knights and fortresses was coming to an end, which contributed to the instability of states that failed to modernize fast enough.

Challenges also arose in international trade. In Northern Europe, the Hanseatic League, a confederation of mostly German-speaking merchant towns, attempted to dominate trade in the Baltic and the North Sea, much to the chagrin of the states around them.

The Northern European countries were generally less badly affected by the Black Death than were some other parts of Europe, such as the Mediterranean region. Nevertheless, even in Scandinavia the crisis had far-reaching consequences. The most striking example is that Norway—previously the most centralized of the three Nordic kingdoms—lost its independence during the late medieval crisis.

In the 1970s, an archaeological study found that up to 40 percent of farms in Norway had been abandoned in the fourteenth century, whereas in other parts of the region fewer farms met this fate, and in Finland and Skåne almost none. These findings must reflect, at least in part, the impact of the Black Death, which is estimated to have caused the deaths of 50–65 percent of the Norwegian population.

Norway's political status also deteriorated: its tradition of separate kingship was broken, and the small Norwegian nobility lost almost all influence. Norwegian monarchy had become dynastically intertwined with that of Sweden in the first decades of the fourteenth century, and then was weakened in a series of unsuccessful wars. In 1380, a union was concluded with Denmark. This union, which remained in place for more than 400 years, had important cultural consequences: even the written Norwegian language died out, and Danish came to be used instead. However, the decline was far from total. Norway's domestic institutions mostly remained in place, and the decline of the Norwegian nobility's influence was at least partially counterbalanced by improvements to the status of Norwegian peasants.

Another part of the Nordic world that experienced far-reaching change during the crisis was Iceland. Although it remained untouched by the Black Death, many Icelandic farms were still abandoned: possibly due to other, more localized, epidemics, or perhaps due to the onset of more intensive fishing. The latter development may also partially explain the abandonment of farms in Norway.

The worst affected Nordic victim of the late medieval crisis, however, was certainly Greenland: the Scandinavian settlement there completely died out by the early sixteenth century. One cause must have been the change in climate, which made shipping to Greenland, and therefore trade with Europe, almost impossible. Another was very likely the Nordic settlers' conflicts with Inuit tribes, whose settlement area spread southward as the climate cooled. The last surviving records of medieval European contact with Greenland date from 1409.

Symptoms of the crisis were also felt in other parts of Scandinavia. Peasants, who suffered the most, left few traces in surviving written sources. Instead, these sources tell us about the reduced income of the upper classes, which suggests the peasantry's situation must have been difficult. But at the same time as poorer nobles saw their incomes fall, richer landowners were able to buy up their land cheaply. Especially in Denmark and Iceland, this meant that the power and wealth of large landowners increased.

Scandinavia was also affected by peasant uprisings, including the Engelbrekt uprising in Sweden in 1434, and rebellions in Norway in 1434–38 and Denmark in 1438–41. All these were suppressed, but in Denmark they contributed to a partial introduction of a form of serfdom, something that would become a recurring feature of the Danish economy, differentiating it from the rest of Scandinavia. In other regions, the few remaining peasants were instead able to bargain for better conditions. Notably, the burdens on Norwegian peasants declined in the fourteenth century—in the Oslo area, for instance, the tithe fell by up to 40 percent between 1300 and 1400.

A major political outcome of the late medieval crisis in Scandinavia was the Kalmar Union, a conglomerate state of all three Scandinavian kingdoms that existed from 1397 to 1523. The complicated story of its establishment goes back to Sweden's successful political consolidation in the mid-thirteenth century, which led Swedish monarchs to seek the expansion of their influence into neighboring countries in the first half of the fourteenth century. In 1332, Swedish king Magnus IV (1316–74) bought up the Danish provinces of Skåne, Halland and Blekinge, which Denmark had mortgaged to fund its unsuccessful campaigns against the Hanseatic League. In 1343, Magnus IV furthermore reached an agreement with Norwegian nobles, whereby his youngest son, Haakon (1340–80), became the next king of Norway. During his son's minority, Magnus ruled as regent, and a union between Norway and Sweden thus temporarily came into being until Haakon VI Magnusson came of age in 1355.

At the same time, Swedish interests in Finland had clashed with those of Novgorod (a region of Russia); in 1323, Sweden and Novgorod signed the Peace of Nöteborg, for the first time demarcating the Swedish–Russian border. Over the course of the fourteenth century, present-day Finland came to be politically integrated with Sweden: indeed, southwestern Finland became one of the central regions of the Swedish state, with its own bishop, important towns and monasteries, and local Swedish-speaking nobility.

In the second half of the century, however, Denmark once again became the dominant state. In 1360, the Danish king Valdemar IV Atterdag (circa 1320–75) recaptured Skåne, and a year later the Swedish island of Gotland, where King Magnus IV was defeated in battle in 1361 or 1362. In 1363, a delegation of Swedish nobles who had been expelled by Magnus after a failed uprising presented an invitation to Albert of Mecklenburg (1338–1412), the second son of King Magnus IV's sister Euphemia and Duke Albert II of Mecklenburg, to take the Swedish throne. Albert then launched a successful military campaign against the supporters of Magnus, who were assisted by Haakon VI, ending with his crowning as the king of Sweden in 1364. The war nevertheless continued for another eight years, and even after the peace treaty, support for Albert remained weak and mostly concentrated in German-dominated towns.

King Valdemar IV Atterdag died in 1375, after a long and successful rule. King Haakon VI of Norway, exhausted by near-constant warfare and prolonged conflict with King Albert of Sweden, passed away five years later. Because Valdemar's daughter Margaret (1387–1412) had married Haakon VI, their five-year-old son, Olaf II (1370–87), was elected king of Denmark, and in 1380 he also inherited the Norwegian throne. Margaret ruled initially as regent for her son, but Olaf II died in 1387, after which Margaret I became the full ruler of both Denmark and Norway. In the same year, the Swedish nobility definitively fell out with King Albert, and the Swedish council of state appealed to Queen Margaret for protection. Margaret then sent her troops to Sweden, and Albert was defeated and overthrown in the same year. Subsequently, Margaret was elected the ruler of Sweden, and all three Scandinavian kingdoms were thus united.

A 1423 effigy of Queen Margaret I of the Kalmar Union, who ruled over Denmark, Norway and Sweden.

In hindsight, it is difficult to say whether the union was meant to last. Margaret seems to have worked purposefully toward the unification of the three kingdoms, but success would have been impossible without the consent of Danish, Norwegian and Swedish nobles. Margaret's legitimacy was for some reason accepted by them all, even though there could have been other pretenders to the throne. In any case, it seems that a part of the agreement was that the new union had to find a suitable king with blood ties to all three dynasties.

ST BRIDGET

In medieval Catholicism, saints were seen as important intermediaries between God and humanity. While they were not worshiped directly, their intercession was believed to amplify the power of prayers, which gave saints a central role in everyday religious life. Relics and pilgrimage sites associated with saints could also provide significant political and economic benefits, much like modern-day tourist attractions.

St Bridget of Sweden (1303–73) was one of the most powerful spiritual figures in medieval Scandinavia. She was born into Swedish nobility: her father, Birger Persson (?–1327), was a prominent lawman in Uppsala, while her mother descended from the powerful Folkung dynasty. After her husband's death, Bridget devoted herself to religious life, experiencing visionary dialogues with Christ and Virgin Mary. She also pursued political influence, using her status and prophecies to mediate in international conflicts such as the Hundred Years' War.

Through royal support, particularly from Magnus IV, Bridget established in 1346 her own abbey in Vadstena. Moving to Rome in 1350, she continued to be involved in Scandinavian affairs and founded the Bridgettine Order, which was approved by the pope in 1370.

Queen Margaret I saw St Bridget's canonisation as a valuable opportunity to win the favour of Vadstena and influential political circles in Sweden. In 1389, she sent a letter to the pope, describing the flow of pilgrims to Vadstena and the miracles occurring at Bridget's tomb. On October 7–8, 1391, Bridget's canonization was solemnly celebrated in Rome.

Such a person was found, and Margaret's nephew Bugislav, known as Eric of Pomerania (1381/2–1459), was crowned king of all three countries in 1397, succeeding Margaret. At Eric's coronation, in the Swedish town of Kalmar, two documents were drafted: the coronation letter and the union letter, which underscored his status as the king of Denmark, Norway and Sweden all at once, emphasizing the idea of unity.

However, continuing trade-related conflicts with the Hanseatic League soon exacerbated internal tensions in the Kalmar Union. The Engelbrekt uprising, in Sweden, led by Swedish nobleman and mine-owner Engelbrekt Engelbrektsson (circa 1390–1436), epitomized this unrest, driven by grievances against both the Hanseatic League and Erik's royal policies. As similar uprisings spread across the union, Danish and Norwegian councils of state also challenged Erik's authority, and he was eventually deposed as king of Denmark and Sweden in 1439. In the same year, the ascension to the throne of his successor, Christopher of Bavaria (1416–48), further symbolized the union's fragility, as Christopher had separate coronations in Denmark, Norway and Sweden. Political strife continued; Christopher's successor, Christian I of Oldenburg (1426–81), was successfully crowned the next king of Denmark and Norway, but Sweden instead elected a local nobleman named Karl Knutsson Bonde (circa 1408–70) as its new king. Most likely, the goal of the Swedish nobles was not to abolish the union altogether, but they were certainly dissatisfied with Danish-German dominance.

In the end, the situation was more one of volatility than determined resistance. Christian I and his son John (1455–1513) both found occasional support in Sweden, while Karl Knutsson Bonde experienced two dethronements. After Bonde's reign, however, no new king was elected, and Sweden instead transitioned to rule by heads of state (*riksföreståndare*) with more limited power. Still, they could yield significant influence: Sweden's Sten Sture the Elder (circa 1440–1503) defeated Christian I's troops in battle in 1471, but he conceded to King John in 1497. In 1501, an uprising against King John broke out in Norway and Sweden, but it succeeded only in the latter, after which Norwegian resistance to the Kalmar Union kings mostly ceased. In Sweden, the office of the head of state passed on to Svante Nilsson (c. 1460–12), Eric Trolle (circa 1460–1529/30) and then Sten Sture the Younger (1493–1520).

Christian II's (1481–1559) ascension to the throne in 1513 sparked further Danish–Swedish conflict, as will be explored in the following chapter. But all in all, by the second half of the fourteenth century, Sweden had become something of an aristocratic republic, favoring nobility over a strong monarch. This, however, did not last. Christian II's controversial reign ultimately led to the nobleman Gustav Vasa's (1496–1560) election as the new king of Sweden in 1523, ending the Kalmar Union and the Scandinavian Middle Ages altogether.

Before its eventual collapse, the Kalmar Union managed to survive for almost 150 years—longer than many other states. It also left some important legacies. Firstly, since the territory it had governed was so large, the Kalmar Union had fostered quite an advanced state apparatus and ideology of the abstract power of the state. In all three countries, the council of state could act as guardian of sovereignty in the absence of the

Kalmar Union king, and Sweden adopted its first official state seal, which made it possible to issue laws even in the king's absence, when the royal seal could not be used. Secondly, new groups in society—including peasants and townspeople—had become politically active during times of turbulence.

The end of the Kalmar Union did not mean a return to the conditions that preceded it. On the contrary, the era of its existence can be described as an important intermediate stage in the transformation of the medieval Scandinavian kingdoms into early modern absolutist states.

7

WARS AND POLITICS: 1500s–1600s

EUROPE'S TRANSITION FROM THE Middle Ages to the early modern period is often characterized as a time of revolutions that brought about major, long-term transformation. The scientific revolution ushered in modern natural sciences, the economic and financial revolution gave rise to international banks and financial markets, the geographical revolution massively expanded the world known to Europeans, and the religious revolution permanently shattered the Catholic unity of Europe. It was also a period when political developments led to the emergence of absolutist monarchies, military innovations brought about the widespread use of firearms, and the traditional power of the nobility began to wane, challenged by an alliance of the monarchy and lower estates.

Oftentimes, these developments reached Scandinavia later than they reached Western Europe, but in some ways, sixteenth- and seventeenth-century Scandinavia was also at the forefront of early modern change, with foreign influences and local conditions coming together in a distinctive trajectory of development. This enabled Sweden and Denmark—the two Scandinavian kingdoms that had survived the late medieval crisis—to play an outsized role in regional and European politics. In Sweden in particular, the seventeenth century has come to be known as "the era of great power" (*Stormaktstiden*), characterized by territorial expansion of the Swedish state on a scale unmatched before or since.

But in the sixteenth century, Sweden and Denmark were already undergoing significant political transformations, as their monarchs sought to reform the still largely medieval states by reining in the power of the established aristocracy, with support from lower nobility, burgeoning middle classes, conscript armies and newly founded state churches. This meant inevitable conflict with the idea of aristocratic constitutionalism, according to which power resided primarily with the council of state, and the king was merely the first among equals. With new assertiveness, early modern monarchs sought to govern alone and personally, abolishing such constraints on their rule.

These tensions first came to a head in Denmark, which faced significant internal strife in the last years of the Kalmar Union, exacerbated by external pressures. Still an elective monarchy, Denmark's succession law dictated that the council of state should elect the new king from among the sons or close male relatives of the previous monarch. When assuming the throne, the new king had to sign a coronation charter, a kind of contract limiting his authority.

Christian II, the last monarch of the Kalmar Union, came into conflict with Danish nobles over the stringent terms of his coronation charter immediately after his coronation in 1513. At the same time, he was also involved in a major external conflict: his attempts to keep the Kalmar Union together had brought him to war with Sweden. By 1520, he managed to subdue Sweden, but then he miscalculated: trying to permanently rid himself of his Swedish opponents, he invited leading members of Swedish noble families to a feast and had them murdered. This event, which became known as the Stockholm Bloodbath, immediately made him very unpopular in Sweden, where he was given the nickname Christian the Tyrant. A rebellion led by Gustav Vasa broke out against his rule.

King Christian II, whom the Swedes called Christian the Tyrant, was the last monarch of the Kalmar Union.

THE REFORMATION

In Scandinavia, the transition from the medieval to the early modern period is associated not with the fall of Constantinople (1453) or Columbus's discovery of America (1492) but with the Reformation and related political changes. Triggered by a late-medieval crisis in the Catholic Church, the Reformation addressed calls for a "purer," less materialistic form of faith that emphasized personal spirituality and the reading of scripture. In the Scandinavian kingdoms, this created conditions for improved literacy, education and development of modern written languages.

In Sweden, the Reformation began in 1527 under King Gustav Vasa, who saw it as a way to strengthen royal power and seize church lands. Still, Lutheran ideas spread gradually, with Sweden establishing its state church over the course of several decades. In 1526, Olaus Petri (1493–1552), a follower of Martin Luther, translated the New Testament into Swedish, which laid the grounds for modern written Swedish.

Denmark and Norway adopted Protestantism in 1536 under Christian III. In Norway, resistance from the church initially delayed reform, but opposition waned after its key figures fled or were ousted. The Danish Bible, published in 1550, was also adopted in Norway, leading to the decline of written Norwegian and its replacement by Danish.

By the late sixteenth century, the Scandinavian monarchs had become the supreme heads of their national churches, integrating religious authority into their rule, and Lutheranism had been established as the dominant faith across the region.

In 1522, a second domestic revolt erupted against Christian II over his attempts to enact reforms that would have loosened the constraints of the coronation charter. His uncle, later Frederick I (1471–1533), emerged as the leader of the rebellion, which in 1523 culminated in Christian II's defeat and Frederick's ascent to the throne. However, upon Frederick's death in 1533, the Catholic Danish nobles initially resisted crowning his Protestant son, Christian III (1503–59). Meanwhile, the German Hanseatic town of Lübeck sought to bolster its influence in Denmark by supporting the reinstatement of Christian II, who remained popular among the common people despite his prior defeat.

These tensions came to a head in the so-called Count's Feud (*Grevens Fejde*), a two-year civil war between the factions supporting Christian II and Christian III respectively. This conflict brought forth deep-seated tensions within Danish society, including the cleavage between those advocating for a strong central government and those opposing it, as well as tensions between nobility and peasantry, Catholics and Lutherans, and Danes and Germans. Ultimately, Christian III emerged victorious, solidifying his rule and making Protestantism the state religion in Denmark. Despite this, Danish nobles retained a significant degree of power, and Denmark remained an elective monarchy for another century.

In 1559, Christian III was succeeded by his son Frederick II (1534–88), whose foreign policy ambitions focused on elevating Denmark's stature and influence in the Baltic region. When he passed away in 1588, his son Christian IV (1577–1648) ascended to the throne at the young age of eleven, with the council of state initially ruling in his stead. But Christian IV went on to reign for fifty-nine years, the longest tenure of any Danish king and, indeed, any Scandinavian monarch. As one of Denmark's most popular kings, he initiated reforms and projects that elevated his kingdom's stability and prosperity. However, his reign was marred by several wars, notably the Thirty Years' War (1618–48), which drained the country's resources.

In the sixteenth century, the Swedish kings attempted to centralize power, transform the nobility into a class of loyal civil servants and use the Reformation to take over the possessions of the church, just as the Danish kings did. However, Swedish kings had an advantage over Danish monarchs: they had succeeded much earlier in adopting a hereditary succession law and did not have to deal with restrictive coronation charters.

After heading the successful rebellion against Christian the Tyrant, Gustav Vasa became the king of Sweden in 1523. Soon after, he also brought the Reformation to Sweden, confiscating all property of the Catholic Church and establishing the Swedish state church as an extension of his personal power. Gustav Vasa also introduced hereditary monarchy, took away most of the influence of the council of state and reorganized the army on the basis of conscription. In many ways, he already governed Sweden as if he was an absolutist ruler. But in all of this, he encountered remarkably little opposition from Swedish nobles, perhaps because most of his likely rivals had been killed in the Stockholm Bloodbath. Gustav Vasa also had his new army with which to quash any possible rebellions and reward his supporters with careers in the military.

THE ASTRONOMER TYCHO BRAHE

The first significant Scandinavian scientist was Tycho Brahe (1546–1601), a Danish nobleman, alchemist, astrologist and astronomer. In his own time, Brahe was best known for revising the Copernican heliocentric theory by proposing a cosmology in which Earth remained immobile, with the sun orbiting it, while other planets orbited the sun. This compromise between geocentricism and heliocentrism remained the official view of the Roman Catholic Church until Galileo's discoveries in 1610.

Brahe's more lasting contributions to the history of science were his extensive and precise astronomical observations, which predated the invention of the telescope. These meticulous measurements later enabled Johannes Kepler to determine that planets orbit the sun in elliptical paths. Among Brahe's other notable discoveries was the supernova in the Cassiopeia constellation in 1572, challenging the Aristotelian belief that heavenly spheres were unchanging and stars could neither appear nor disappear.

Brahe owned an estate on the Danish island of Hven, where between 1576 and 1580 he built his Uraniborg observatory. Named after Urania, the muse of astronomy, Uraniborg resembled a small fortress and included observatory towers, a library, royal guest rooms, student living quarters and an alchemical laboratory. Its construction was extraordinarily costly, consuming about 1 percent of the Danish national budget in the years it was built—a proportion greater than the United States allocated to the Apollo space program.

In 1597, due to the depletion of public funds, Brahe had to abandon Hven, and he died four years later. During his last two years, he mentored Johannes Kepler, who made use of Brahe's data to formulate the laws of planetary motion.

Gustav Vasa of Sweden introduced hereditary monarchy and governed Sweden almost like an absolutist ruler.

When Gustav Vasa passed away in 1560, his eldest son, Eric XIV (1533–77), succeeded him, but immediately faced significant challenges. In part, this was due to his own impulsive nature, but it was also because his father had granted semi-autonomous duchies to his three half-brothers, giving them considerable power. The most influential half-brother was Duke Johan of Finland (1537–92), who had solidified his position by marrying Catherine Jagiellon (1526–83), the sister of the Polish king Sigismund August. Johan's alliance with Poland put him on a collision course with Eric XIV, who in 1562 sent an army to Finland and had Duke Johan arrested and imprisoned. But Eric XIV's erratic behaviour also alienated Swedish nobility, and his personally mandated execution of some members of the noble Sture family in 1567 sparked a rebellion that resulted in Eric XIV's deposition in 1569 and

Duke Johan's becoming the king of Sweden as John III.

Compared to his half-brother, John III was a cautious ruler who sought to maintain the support of Swedish nobles despite his Catholic faith and marriage to a Polish noblewoman. Nevertheless, he faced competition from his brother Duke Karl (1550–1611), who wielded considerable influence in the Swedish provinces of Södermanland, Närke and Värmland.

Upon Johan III's death in 1592, his son Sigismund (1566–1632), who had been the king of Poland since 1587, inherited the Swedish throne. Initially, he attempted to rule both countries and restore Sweden to Catholicism. However, when faced with staunch opposition from Swedish nobles and clergy, Sigismund ultimately acquiesced to Sweden remaining Protestant, and appointed Duke Karl as his regent. Subsequently, Duke Karl moved to undermine Sigismund's authority, which led to armed conflict and Sigismund's defeat in 1598. In 1604, Duke Carl ascended to the Swedish throne as king Charles IX, solidifying the Vasa dynasty's control over Sweden.

By that time, regional politics were firmly focused on the Swedish–Danish relationship, which in the sixteenth century can be divided into three distinct stages. From approximately 1500 to 1523, the relations were characterized by conflict, with Denmark ultimately failing to prevent Sweden's secession from the Kalmar Union. During the second period, about 1523 to 1560, Denmark and Sweden enjoyed a period of relative peace and cooperation. Finally, these dynamics shifted drastically around 1560, marking the onset of a prolonged rivalry between Denmark and Sweden over dominance of the Baltic Sea.

The backdrop of this rivalry was the uncertain status of the region known as Old Livonia, on the other side of the Baltic Sea. Comprising present-day Estonia and Latvia, the area had for several centuries been controlled by the knightly Teutonic Order of the Holy Roman Empire. By the mid-fifteenth century, however, the Order's increasingly obvious military weaknesses had sparked a competition among various proximate regional powers that included Sweden, Denmark, Poland and Russia. These tensions first peaked in the late 1550s, and they culminated in the inconclusive Nordic Seven Years' War, initiated by Denmark in 1563. Ultimately, Sweden managed to outmaneuver Denmark, with Danish kings relinquishing their claim on Old Livonia in 1575.

Nevertheless, Danish–Swedish rivalry persisted into the seventeenth century, resulting in frequent wars against each other, but also against Poland and Russia, and interventions in the wars of Continental Europe, notably the Thirty Years' War. For Scandinavian monarchs, the wars provided an opportunity for further centralization of power. In 1648, the Danish king Christian IV was succeeded by his son Frederick III (1609–70), who continued the wars against Sweden and, in 1660, managed to establish absolute monarchy in Denmark and Norway. The wars continued under his successor, Christian V (1646–99), who ascended to the throne in 1670 and is known for his unsuccessful bid to reclaim the province of Skåne from Sweden, a costly and ultimately fruitless endeavor. His son Frederick IV (1671–1730) assumed the Danish and Norwegian thrones in 1699, reigning during the Great Northern War of 1700–21, during which Sweden was finally and conclusively defeated.

In Sweden, Charles IX, as the opponent of Catholic Sigismund, steadfastly championed the Protestant cause, which was even more true of his successor, Gustavus Adolphus (1594–1632), who became the king in 1611. He propelled Sweden to military dominance in the Thirty Years' War, earning wide renown as a military commander, despite his early death in 1632 at the Battle of Lützen, in Germany.

At the time, Gustavus Adolphus's only surviving legitimate child, Queen Christina (1626–89), was still underage, so the council of state governed in her stead until 1644. Famous as one of the most educated European women of the 1600s, Queen Christina stirred controversy by opting not to marry, and further scandalized Swedish society by abdicating her throne in 1654, converting to Catholicism and eventually relocating to Rome. Her successor, Charles X Gustav (1622–60), gained

Queen Christina governed Sweden for over twenty years before abdicating the throne and relocating to Rome. Pope Alexander VII described Christina as "a queen without a realm, a Christian without faith and a woman without shame."

renown for his successful March Across the Belts in early 1658: a crossing of the frozen straits of the Baltic Sea to launch a surprise attack on Danish islands. His reign was followed by that of Charles XI (1655–97), who introduced absolutism, following the Danish example, and subsequently Charles XII (1682–1718), the last Swedish king of the Great Power Era, who commanded Swedish forces in the Great Northern War.

As already noted, the early modern era was a period of rapid modernization, when increasingly obsolete political and societal structures were replaced with new and more efficient ones, disadvantaging states that had failed to establish a strong system of central government. Significantly, this included most of the Holy Roman Empire, and not least its Baltic lands, the decline of which fueled Swedish–Danish rivalry. Conversely, among the winners were the states that centralized and built effective bureaucracies early, temporarily giving them outsized military influence. Denmark and, especially, Sweden were some of the most impressive examples of this development.

The Scandinavian kingdoms needed reliable state bureaucracies because constant wars needed armies, and armies needed soldiers and supplies. An effective state apparatus could collect taxes, recruit young men into the army, punish those who tried to evade taxes or recruitment, and prevent coups or rebellions. Remarkably, early modern Scandinavian commoners put up minimal resistance. One factor may have been their fear of serfdom, prevalent in other parts of Europe at the time—they possibly viewed taxation and military service as a preferable alternative. Another factor must have been state-mandated coercion.

In Sweden, the process of making governance more effective had in some ways already begun during the reign of Gustav Vasa, but its defining moment came during the reign of Gustavus Adolphus and his chancellor, Axel Oxenstierna (1583–1654). In the years 1610–30, Sweden developed a network of royal officials and civil servants covering the entire Swedish territory. These officials were professional, salaried and replaceable, with clear responsibilities and job descriptions, and their reach and effectiveness had no equal in Europe.

At the central state level, Oxenstierna created several colleges (*collegia*) akin to modern ministries and departments, each responsible for an area of governance, such as domestic or foreign policy, finance, land army, navy, mining, trade and industry, or justice. The heads of the colleges were given seats in the council of state, which thereby came to resemble a modern cabinet. This greatly added to Sweden's state capacity. A similar system emerged in Denmark.

This newfound efficiency came in very handy during the constant wars involving the two Scandinavian kingdoms in the seventeenth century. Of particular importance was the Thirty Years' War, which had initially erupted as a Protestant uprising against the Holy Roman Emperor but soon evolved into broader religious and political struggle across Europe.

Denmark's Christian IV at first opted to support the Protestant cause against the emperor, but soon faced defeat, with Jutland falling under the control of the emperor's forces by 1626. Sweden, initially preoccupied with conflicts across the Baltic against Poland, joined the fray in 1630, under the leadership of Gustavus Adolphus. Despite the king's untimely death in battle, Sweden's campaign in northern Germany proved highly successful and led to the capture of substantial territories.

In 1643, Sweden built on this success by successfully attacking Denmark, which by then had aligned itself with the emperor. Under the Treaty of Brömsebro in 1645, which ended that conflict, Sweden acquired several Danish territories, including the Baltic islands of Saaremaa (Ösel) and Gotland. Moreover, the 1648 Peace of Westphalia, which concluded the Thirty Years' War, allowed Sweden to consolidate its territorial gains in northern Germany and conclusively establish itself as the preeminent military power in the Baltic Sea region. Neither treaty, however, meant that the Danish–Swedish rivalry was over. Smaller-scale conflicts between the two continued, with Sweden gaining more Danish territory on the southern half of the Scandinavian Peninsula.

The final war of the period was the Great Northern War of 1700–21, which conclusively ended Sweden's stint as a great power. In it, Sweden, led by king Charles XII, had to fight a coalition of Denmark, Brandenburg, Poland and Russia. Even though Sweden's armies proved to be effective, and a major victory over much larger Russian forces was scored in the Battle of Narva in 1700, the war ended with Sweden being outnumbered and defeated. Under the Peace of Nystad (Uusikaupunki in Finnish), Sweden thus had to give up its possession of Ingria, Livonia, Estonia and a large part of Karelia, which all went to Russia. The same happened to its northern German lands, with some going to Brandenburg, and other parts to Poland. In the end, of all the overseas possessions it had gained in the previous two centuries, Sweden only managed to hold on to a small part of Pomerania and the German town of Wismar.

Denmark once again failed to regain any lost territory, but it gained something else: Sweden withdrew its support for rivals of the Danish king, the dukes of Holstein-Gottorp, in Jutland, and agreed to give up its right to collect customs in Öresund—the narrow strait between Sweden and Denmark—which had long been a point of contention between the two states.

By the early eighteenth century, both Sweden and Denmark had become second-rate powers, having lost their competitive edge to other states in the region—particularly Russia.

THE MYSTERIOUS DEATH AND AFTERLIFE OF CHARLES XII

On November 30, 1718, the thirty-six-year-old king of Sweden, Charles XII, was shot dead during what was to be his last invasion of Norway. He was inspecting the trenches of his army during a siege of the Norwegian fortress Fredrikshald (Halden) when a mysterious projectile hit him in the head, killing him instantly. Almost as instantly, rumors started circulating that someone on his own side had shot him—possibly because he was tired of the king's absolutist rule, which seemed to drag Sweden into endless wars. Although unverified, the rumors nevertheless reflected society's changing mood: a form of absolutism fatigue that set the scene for Sweden's subsequent turn to parliamentary rule.

A popular, if unlucky, figure, Charles XII went on to occupy a prominent position in Swedish collective memory in the centuries that followed, particularly in right-wing nationalist circles. Founded in 1910, the Carolinian Association (Karolinska Förbundet) was dedicated to the study and preservation of Swedish history during this era, but in its early years it also had a political mission, summarized by its first chairman, Prince Carl, as

> to contribute to a revival in the nation of the spirit that once inspired the men of the Carolinian era—not the warlike spirit that sought out great feats and adventures, but rather that side of the Carolinian spirit which proved capable of shaping characters: self-sacrificing, hardened men, whose steadfast resilience no misfortune could bend, and whose elevated and brilliant qualities are truly worthy of admiration and emulation by the Swedish people.

8

THE EARLY MODERN PERIOD: ABSOLUTISM AND PARLIAMENTARISM

THE DEVELOPMENTS THAT LED TO the death of Charles XII in 1718 had resulted from a remarkable interplay between the domestic and international rivalries that helped to turn the kingdoms of Sweden and Denmark into some of the strongest and most modern European states of their time. The main domestic rivalry that facilitated this process was an old one: that between the monarch and the nobility. After setbacks in the first half of the sixteenth century, the Danish and Swedish nobles regained their strength in the following decades, with their power reaching a historic apotheosis in the beginning and middle of the seventeenth century. Their political ideal was a form of mixed rule, where power would have been shared between the king and the council of state, controlled by the high nobility.

However, such mixed rule was inherently unstable, as the allocation of resources needed for warfare created constant strife between the monarch and the council. Scandinavia was not unique in this respect. In most large European countries, the rulers were eventually able to dissolve similar councils and start ruling personally as absolutist sovereign rulers.

King Charles XII was the last Swedish king of the Great Power Era.

In Denmark, this happened when a Diet of Estates (*Stændermødet*)—a kind of ad hoc parliament—was convened in 1660 to deal with the financial crisis that had followed a costly war with Sweden. On this occasion, the Diet's representatives of clergy and townspeople professed their loyalty to the king and proposed that Frederick III enact the law of hereditary succession on the condition that the nobility would also be made to pay taxes. Under further pressure from the army loyal to the king, the nobles capitulated to these demands, and Frederick was declared the sole sovereign ruler of Denmark. This meant a dramatic increase in the power of the king, as he no longer had to consider the views of the council of state on the question of his successor.

After that, both the Danish council of state and the *Stændermødet* itself were dissolved, and the king's absolutist rule was confirmed in a separate law (*Kongeloven*) in 1665, making Denmark the only European kingdom with an actual written absolutist constitution. The law stipulated that the only two things the king was not allowed to do were to decrease his own power and to give up the Lutheran faith.

As a form of compensation for lost influence, the Danish nobles now gained more power over their tenants, as tax collection and conscription into the army were made a prerogative of landowners. In the end, it was thus the peasants who bore the hardest burden of absolutism: they lost all direct contact with the state and were largely at the mercy of their landowners.

The newly absolutist Denmark was strong enough to pose a serious threat to Sweden in the following Scanian War (1675–79). Although Sweden successfully resisted Denmark, at the conclusion of the war it found itself in much the same situation as its enemy had been in before: the state coffers were empty, and lower estates demanded that either the land holdings of nobles be reduced, or the nobles be forced to contribute by paying taxes.

In the end, the nobles had to do both, because during the convening of the *Riksdag* (the Swedish equivalent of the *Stændermødet*) in 1680, King Charles XI also managed to leverage the support of lower estates to change the council of state from a governing organ into a privy council of the king. This move was also supported by the lower nobility, mainly officers and civil servants, who did not own much land.

As an absolutist ruler, Charles XI then went on to confiscate much of the land that his predecessors had liberally handed out to nobles as rewards for their service. In the 1680s, the Swedish nobility's land holdings were reduced by one third, and the king was accused of overreaching. Swedish absolutism nevertheless survived and culminated in the rule of the following king, Charles XII. However, as Sweden's resources were depleted in the Great Northern War, it seems that many Swedes were already thoroughly tired of absolutism by the time Charles XII was killed in Fredriksten.

At the same time, there were limits to what absolutism could do. All European states at the time, including Sweden and Denmark, were conglomerate states, consisting of different territories, mainly held together by military force or the threat thereof. But all these territories nevertheless had their own laws, customs, privileges and societal hierarchies that the central government had to respect, at least to some extent. Although absolutist monarchs were striving for unity, the new institutions of governance were mostly placed on top of and alongside the already existing ones. This made, for instance, Danish rule in Norway, Iceland, the Faroe Islands and the duchies of Schleswig and Holstein, as well as in Denmark itself, very different.

Furthermore, absolutism could create expectations that could not be met. When Iceland experienced a major volcanic eruption in 1783, with massive flows of lava and fallout of poisonous volcanic ash, it looked to the Danish king for assistance, but he arguably lacked both the will and capacity to provide it. The situation in the duchies of Schleswig and Holstein, located in the southern part of the Jutland Peninsula, was another pressing concern. Schleswig and Holstein had a mixed population of Danes and Germans, and their legal status within the Danish kingdom remained a subject of contention and security risk, which absolutism did little to alleviate.

Sweden, which acquired significant new territories in the sixteenth and seventeenth centuries, treated its recently conquered lands not as full parts of the state but as something more akin to colonial possessions. The nobles of Estonia or Livonia, for example, were not represented in the Swedish council of state or *Riksdag*. The only exceptions were the provinces conquered from Denmark on the Scandinavian peninsula itself, which were indeed fully integrated, but achieving that could take decades, as was the case in Skåne and Bohuslän, where the strong local nobility was eventually able to defend their customs and privileges. Therefore, even though Danish and Swedish monarchs succeeded in establishing absolutist rule in their core states, they were still very dependent on local circumstances in more peripheral parts of their kingdoms.

In Sweden's case, most of this legal and political diversity eventually went away with its defeat in the Great Northern War and the subsequent loss of nearly all of its recently acquired territories. Nor did its territory increase substantially in the eighteenth century, which, in comparison to the sixteenth and seventeenth centuries, proved a much more peaceful time, when Scandinavia experienced sustained economic and population growth and improved living standards.

SCIENTIFIC ACHIEVEMENTS IN THE SEVENTEENTH AND EIGHTEENTH CENTURIES

Early modern Swedish expansionism in the Baltic region, and its wide-reaching administrative reforms, came with a renewed emphasis on education. This included the founding of new universities in Tartu (1632), Turku (1640) and Lund (1666). Uppsala University also expanded significantly, becoming a regional intellectual and cultural hub, alongside the University of Copenhagen, in Denmark.

Prominent Scandinavian scholars such as Olof Rudbeck (1630–1702), at Uppsala, and Thomas Bartholin (1616–80), at Copenhagen, made significant scientific advances, including the discovery of the lymphatic system. Which scholar discovered it first continues to be disputed between the two institutions.

Rudbeck also made significant contributions to the study of Swedish plants, laying the foundation for a botanic tradition that subsequently flourished in Sweden under Carl Linnaeus (Carl von Linné, 1707–78). Linnaeus's work in taxonomy and classification of flora and fauna made him one of the most influential scientists of the eighteenth century. His system for naming species, Systema Naturae, is still used today. Linnaeus also had many students and supervised more than 180 dissertations, earning him international fame and the unwavering loyalty of his disciples.

Even some of the early modern Scandinavian monarchs were interested in intellectual pursuits: not least Queen Christina, who invited the famous French philosopher René Descartes to stay at her court in Sweden. Upon his arrival, he caught a bad cold in the damp Swedish castle and unfortunately soon died.

At the same time, both Scandinavian kingdoms came to experience a degree of internal turmoil in the eighteenth century, as the ideas of the Enlightenment gained a foothold, and new demands for greater political and personal freedoms arose. While Sweden was characterized by pendulum movements between absolutism and parliamentary rule, Danish absolutism experienced a long and painful decline.

The Danish kings who came after Frederick IV did not seriously attempt to take charge of all aspects of governance, and their advisers and the heads of the colleges played an ever more important role. The kings also had their own personal issues. Christian VI (1699–1746), who was crowned in 1730, was very religious and less interested in earthly matters, whereas his successor, Frederick V (1723–66), was an alcoholic and almost incapable of ruling. The limited capacity of the Danish state to keep up with the changing times was also exemplified by the introduction of a form of serfdom (*Stavnsbånd*) in the 1730s, meant to counter the threat of increasing urbanization by bonding Danish peasants between the ages of fourteen and thirty-six to live on the estate where they were born.

Danish absolutism experienced an even deeper crisis when Frederick V's successor, Christian VII (1749–1808), became king in 1766. He had a mental illness that made him unable to govern, and so, for a while, Denmark's actual head of state, and a gray eminence, was the king's personal physician, Johann Friedrich Struensee (1737–72). Influenced by Enlightenment ideals, Struensee enacted many liberal reforms, but paid for them with his life when he was finally arrested and executed in 1772. Still, the new government of the king's relatives and conservative civil servants left absolutism in place, forcing mentally ill Christian VII to sign many documents that he likely did not understand. In 1784, he was made to sign a decree by which he handed over his kingdom to Crown Prince Frederik (1768–1839), who became King Frederick VI in 1808.

Johann Friedrich Struensee was the personal physician of King Christian VII of Denmark. When illness prevented Christian VII from governing, Struensee acted as head of state.

In Sweden, by contrast, a new constitution adopted after Charles XII's death was meant to ensure that absolutism would never return. The king was reduced to the role of the speaker of the council of state, and the council itself, headed by the chancellor, became the governing institution of the state. The *Riksdag* had a similarly important role, having the right to initiate votes of no confidence in members of the council and force them to abdicate. This meant that a balance of power had come into being between the two—similar to that which exists between a modern government and modern parliament. Nevertheless, even though the *Riksdag* now functioned as a forum for political discussions, voting still took place by estate, with each having a single vote.

In Swedish history, this period came to be known as "the time of freedom" (*Frihetstiden*), meaning freedom from absolutist rule. Two embryonic parties developed: Chancellor Arvid Horn (1664–1742) and his supporters in parliament became known as Caps (supported mostly by the lower estates), and their opponents were called Hats (supported by the nobility). However, only some members of the *Riksdag* belonged to these parties, and the parties had no presence outside of parliament. They also did not have clear political ideologies; the main difference between them was that the Hats supported a new war against Russia, with the intention of retaking the territories lost in 1721. After gaining the upper hand in parliament in the late 1730s, the Hats indeed started such a war, which ended with a Swedish defeat and a peace treaty in 1743, causing the loss of further territory to Russia.

The Swedish monarchs during the early and mid-eighteenth century were Queen Ulrika Eleonora (1688–1741) and two kings: Frederick I (1676–1751), who ascended to the throne when his wife Ulrika Eleonora abdicated, and Adolf Frederick (1710–71), a bishop of Lübeck, who descended from Gustav Vasa on his mother's side and whose coronation was supported by Russia after Sweden's defeat in the "The War of the Hats."

The Hats survived the unlucky war against Russia, but their rule finally ended with Sweden's unsuccessful participation in the Seven Years' War (1756–63) as a member of the coalition led by France against Britain and Prussia. The Swedish army was defeated in Prussia, the war caused great inflation in the Swedish economy, and once again relations with Russia worsened. The Caps took over, and some significant liberal reforms were enacted, including the 1766 *Freedom of the Press Act*, which guaranteed public access to official records. Yet the Caps' time in power was limited. In August 1772, the son of King Adolf Frederick, Gustav III (1746–92), assumed the Swedish throne and orchestrated an absolutist coup d'état, with the support of the army and conservative nobles who had grown fearful of the radical ideas of the Enlightenment. After gaining power, Gustav III dissolved the two political parties, strengthened censorship and constrained the power of the *Riksdag*.

However, Gustav III's rule was plagued by discontent, especially on the part of peasants who were fearful of the deterioration of their rights, as state-owned land again started to move into the hands of the nobility. In hope that it would improve Sweden's domestic situation, Gustav III decided to start yet another war against Russia in 1788. However, his plan to conquer Saint Petersburg failed due to the opposition of his own army, and when Denmark came to Russia's help, Gustav III brought his troops back home. The war nevertheless dragged on until Gustav III was murdered in 1792 by a group of conspirators. Still, there was no immediate change to the Swedish constitution, and Gustav III's son Gustav IV Adolf (1778–1837) went on governing in the same absolutist fashion.

THE ENLIGHTENMENT PUBLIC SPHERE IN SCANDINAVIA

Thanks to the influence of Enlightenment ideals in the eighteenth century, literacy and writing flourished in the Nordic countries like never before. Previously, religious texts predominated, but now there were a growing number of secular publications. Iceland, for instance, saw its first non-religious printing press established in 1772. The press published useful texts on subjects such as animal husbandry and household economy, but also books for entertainment. Similar trends took place across the Nordic region, where learning was increasingly put in the service of practical need and economic development, and cheaper printing costs even allowed for the production of lowbrow entertainment.

The eighteenth century also witnessed the rise of newspapers and magazines, enabling wider dissemination of news and social debate. Notable publications included *Stockholms-Posten* in Sweden and the Danish cultural journal *Minerva*. Discussions also took place in cafés, clubs and salons as a new form of middle-class socialization. By the late eighteenth century, such venues were common even in smaller towns, creating a public sphere that was outside the control of the church and state, and aligned with the Enlightenment goal of improving the living standard and moral quality of the people through free debate.

Criticism of state policies often formed part of political discussion, such as Icelandic complaints about the Danish trade monopoly and Norwegian demands for the establishment of their own university and bank. Such criticism was risky, and often subject to censorship attempts, exacerbating the emerging cleavage between conservative and liberal political stances.

9

ECONOMY, TRADE AND COLONIALISM IN THE 1700s

AROUND 1720, A PERIOD OF economic growth began in Scandinavia, subsequently accelerating in the decades of the mid-eighteenth century. Drawing on new Enlightenment ideas about economy and international trade, Sweden and Denmark attempted to proactively capitalize on favorable conditions and ushered in changes in economic policy. Especially for Denmark, this created an era of relatively profitable overseas colonialism, the most lasting outcome of which was the reintegration of Greenland into the Nordic sphere of political and economic influence.

The eighteenth century was also a prosperous period for maritime trade in Europe, especially during the wars between Great Britain and France, when neutral Denmark and Sweden could capture a significant portion of the international shipping market and offer "flags of convenience" to foreign merchant ships. The late eighteenth century is therefore considered the golden age of Danish commerce and navigation, as enterprising merchants could earn substantial profits without much initial capital. Danish vessels sailed only to a limited extent to and from Denmark. Primarily, they provided transportation services to third countries, which could sometimes have unexpected consequences. In 1768, for instance, the Copenhagen merchant Niels Ryberg (1725–1804) managed to establish a trading post in Tórshavn in the Faroe Islands for clandestine trade with Great Britain, resulting in a sudden economic boom for the town that lasted for two decades.

Another asset to Denmark's economic growth was the economy of Norway, which had long been oriented toward Western European exports. By the late seventeenth century, Great Britain had already replaced the Netherlands as Norway's most important trading partner, and the Industrial Revolution, which began in England and Scotland in the eighteenth century, subsequently increased demand for Norwegian timber, fish and iron. Great Britain was likewise a significant trading partner for Sweden, purchasing its iron, tar and oats.

Both in Denmark and Sweden, economic policy was initially directed toward strictly state-controlled economic growth: regulations were put in place to steer production and shipping, and large sums of state funds were allocated to subsidize enterprises. In Iceland, for instance, starting from 1752, the Danish state invested significantly in promoting local economic activity, under the leadership of Sheriff Skúli Magnússon (1711–94). Icelandic merchants and landowners established a joint-stock trading company that received substantial state support; in Reykjavík, a textile manufactory was established for production of Icelandic woolen cloth; workshops were built for sulfur production; and new methods of agriculture and fishing were promoted. However, this activity was not sustainable without the subsidies, and the state's patience eventually ran out. In the 1760s and 1770s, most of these enterprises ceased operations, with the only lasting result being that Reykjavík, the future capital of Iceland, had grown into a tiny settlement.

This and other instances of economic failure were not merely local or regional phenomena: in the 1760s, the international economy worsened and programs of state support for enterprises had to be terminated. The following period was instead characterized by agricultural reforms and cautious liberalization of trade. In 1787, Denmark abolished its state monopoly of trade with Iceland, and a year later did the same for trade with Norway. Henceforth, all subjects of the Danish king could freely exchange goods with each other—although not yet with foreign countries. Starting in 1788, Danish serfdom was also gradually abolished, with resulting benefits to social mobility and Denmark's economic development.

In Sweden, Gustav III implemented similar liberalizing economic reforms, doing away with regulations on grain trade and allowing a certain degree of religious freedom for foreign merchants, which was hoped would bring more foreign capital and expertise to Sweden.

Alongside other forms of economic intervention, investments in transoceanic trade were also introduced. In 1731, the Swedish East India Company was founded in Gothenburg, and in 1784 Sweden acquired the Caribbean island of Saint Barthélemy from France, in exchange for trading privileges in Gothenburg. The island provided a source of fresh water for passing ships, produced moderate amounts of goods such as cotton, sugar, cocoa and tobacco, and promised substantial revenue from trade through its natural harbor. A large proportion of the island's population were enslaved Africans. By the end of the century, its port of Gustavia, named after Gustav III, was visited by around 1330 ships annually. In 1812, the island became private property of the king, but in the mid-1840s it was again taken under national administration. Around the same time, the Swedish parliament abolished slave trading and slavery on Saint Barthélemy.

In terms of colonial trade, the Danes held an edge over the Swedes: Danish colonies in West Africa and the East and West Indies were numerous and expanded over time. They served as bases for relatively extensive trade, including slave trade, although not on a scale comparable to that of the major European powers of the time. In the Caribbean, the Danish West Indies (now the Virgin Islands), annexed or bought from France in 1672, 1718 and 1733, played a significant role in the transatlantic trade: Danish merchants exported firearms and other manufactured goods to Africa in exchange for slaves, who were then transported to the Virgin Islands to work the sugar plantations, enabling Denmark to benefit from commodities such as sugar, rum and molasses.

In the East Indies, Denmark had an important trading post in Tranquebar (now Tharangambadi) on the east coast of the Indian mainland, which also served as a center for Danish missionary efforts. Tranquebar's industrial hinterland provided cotton textiles for export to the European market, as well as exotic spices, coffee and sugar for Denmark. In West

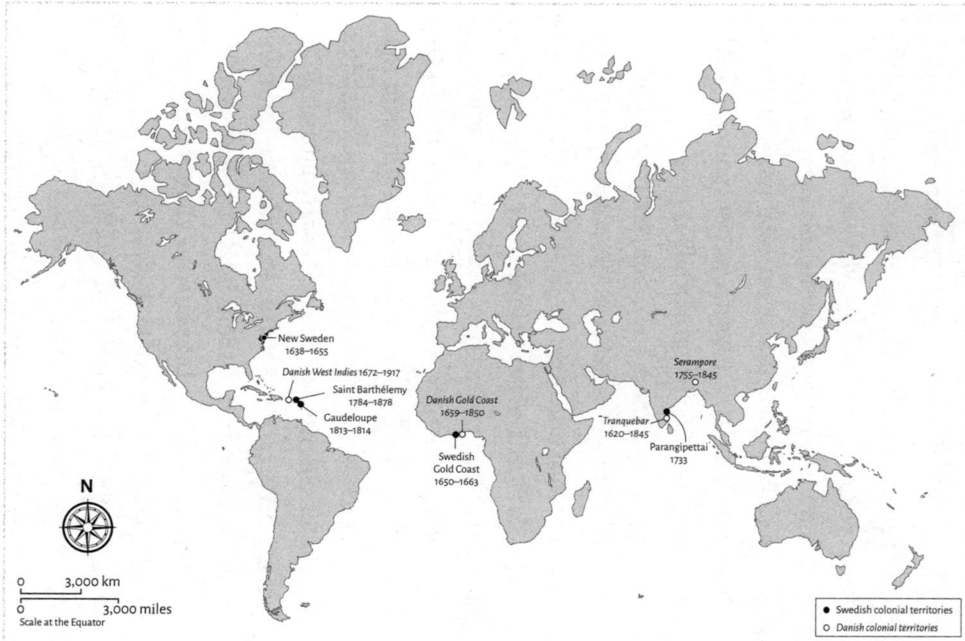

The Scandinavian kingdoms acquired a number of colonies in Africa, Asia and the Americas during their expansionist periods in the seventeenth and eighteenth centuries.

Africa, Danish trading posts and forts comprised the so-called Danish Gold Coast (roughly in present-day southeast Ghana), which engaged in trade in gold, ivory and slaves. In 1792, Denmark banned the slave trade, but the law only took effect in 1803, and an illegal slave trade continued well into the nineteenth century.

Fishing, whaling and trade in the North Atlantic was also attractive for the Danish state, and promised significant profits. At the same time, it faced competition from the English, French and Dutch, who had been whaling off the coast of Greenland and Newfoundland since the seventeenth century. For its part, Denmark could and did assert its legal rights in the North Atlantic, drawing on the historical fact that Greenland had been under the Norwegian crown since the thirteenth century and had become part of the Danish kingdom, along with all other Norwegian possessions, after the dissolution of the Kalmar Union. In the 1660s, the figure of the polar bear was added to the Danish coat of arms as a reminder that Greenland belonged to the Danish realm.

The fate of previous generations of Scandinavian settlers in Greenland was initially unknown to the Danish state. Believing that a settlement might still exist but would need to be converted to Protestantism, Bergen merchants and a Dano-Norwegian priest named Hans Egede (1686–1758) finally organized an expedition to Greenland in 1721, merging commercial interests with religious motives. Once there, they found no Catholic Scandinavians, only Inuit tribes engaged in hunting and fishing, and with no knowledge of Christianity. Subsequently, great efforts were made to spread literacy and convert the Inuit. In 1742, the first Greenlandic catechism was printed, creating a precedent for the use of Greenlandic written language. Still, not all Inuit converted, and most of them continued to live according to their traditional ways, with many having no contact with Europeans at all.

The Danish trading initiatives in Greenland also had limited success. The first company established for trade with Greenland soon had to cease operations. In 1774, a new trading company, KGH (Kongelige Grønlandske Handel), was founded, and Greenland was closed for trade to merchants from other countries. Nevertheless, trade contacts with it remained limited to a few trading posts in southwest Greenland, and, even there, trade was purely based on barter. In the end, the most significant outcome of Denmark's re-engagement with Greenland was the lasting success in the assertion of its territorial rights there.

The eighteenth-century period of overseas economic expansionism came to an end when the two Scandinavian kingdoms of Sweden and Denmark were drawn into the Napoleonic Wars in the early nineteenth century. By that time, their warm-water colonies had grown increasingly unprofitable, especially after the official abolishment of slavery in the late 1840s. Tranquebar, which had already entered economic decline in the 1770s, was sold in 1845 to the British, along with another Danish trading post, Serampore, in Bengal. The Danish Gold Coast outposts were all sold to the same buyer in 1850. Sweden sold Saint Barthélemy back to France in 1878. Only the Virgin Islands remained in Danish hands, until they were sold to the United States in 1917.

THE DANISH ARABIA EXPEDITION

The Danish Arabia Expedition (1761–67) stands as one of the most ambitious scientific explorations of eighteenth-century Europe. It was commissioned by Frederick V of Denmark to expand European knowledge of the Arabian Peninsula. Led by the German mathematician and cartographer Carsten Niebuhr (1733–1815), the team included several Danish, Swedish and German scholars who embarked on a challenging journey from Copenhagen through Egypt to Yemen, facing intense heat, disease and logistical setbacks.

Niebuhr, who was the only member of the expedition to survive malaria and other illnesses, managed to complete substantial portions of the journey alone, even learning Arabic to communicate with locals and better document his findings. Returning to Denmark in 1767, he published his findings in *Description of Arabia* (1772) and *Travels through Arabia and Other Countries in the East* (1774–78). His recording of Arabian astronomical and mathematical knowledge helped to correct European misconceptions, and his meticulous maps and observations of the Arabian Peninsula's geography proved invaluable to future explorers. His books also included some of the first European accounts of Arabian plants, animals and social customs. Finally, Niebuhr's legacy endured in his methodical approach to exploration, which became a model for subsequent scientific expeditions.

10

THE NAPOLEONIC WARS AND THE SWEDISH-NORWEGIAN UNION

IN THE EIGHTEENTH CENTURY, the most important political developments in Scandinavia had involved philosophical, rather than territorial, changes: the supremacy of the upper classes had become contested by the Enlightenment, and Sweden's experiments with parliamentarism had demonstrated that absolutism was not the only viable political system. In the nineteenth century, however, the clashing politics of the great European powers, along with the political and military failures of the Scandinavian kingdoms themselves, once again led to interstate war and significant territorial change. At the same time, domestic developments in Scandinavia resulted in further relaxation of its absolutist and illiberal political orders.

By the time Napoleon Bonaparte took power in France in 1799, the French Revolutionary Wars had already had an impact on all European states and prompted their consolidation in blocs of alliances. Initially, the two Scandinavian kingdoms intended to maintain their neutrality for the benefit of trade. Hence, in 1800 they joined the pro–free trade Neutral League that had been initiated by Russia. However, the League was formed in response to Britain's blockade of French ports, which had hindered neutral shipping. This made the Scandinavian countries, even unintentionally, potential enemies of Britain.

Consequently, in 1801, the British dispatched a fleet, led by Admiral Horatio Nelson, to the Baltic Sea, where it attacked the Danish fleet, near Copenhagen, on April 2. The Danes put up a tough resistance, but in the end faced defeat. Nevertheless, they did not retaliate. The assassination of Russian emperor Paul I and the ascension to the throne of pro-British tsar Alexander I persuaded Crown Prince Frederik to instead make peace with Britain. Furthermore, Sweden had failed to provide aid to Denmark as it had promised, opting instead to sign a peace treaty with the British. From Sweden's point of view, its new alliance with Britain eased the potential threat from Russia. A peace treaty was therefore signed between Denmark and the United Kingdom, involving concessions that allowed profitable wartime trade to continue.

In 1805, King Gustav IV Adolf of Sweden joined the so-called Third Coalition, an alliance the United Kingdom, Russia and Austria had formed against Napoleon. This decision quickly led to clashes between French and Swedish troops in the northern German region of Pomerania, which was still under Swedish control. Despite assistance from the United Kingdom, this episode ended in Sweden's defeat, weakening Gustav IV Adolf's authority. Meanwhile,

French victories at Jena and Auerstadt, in October 1806, solidified Napoleon's power in Germany, and Russia's defeat at Friedland, in June 1807, left Sweden isolated. By the autumn, the French had driven Swedish forces out of Germany entirely, compelling Sweden to conclude a ceasefire with France.

The situation worsened when, in July 1807, France and Russia signed the first of the Treaties of Tilsit, under which Russia was tasked with pressuring Sweden to join Napoleon's Continental System, which aimed to block British access to European ports. The treaty also contained a secret additional protocol granting Russia a free hand in Finland in exchange for its assistance to France against Sweden. Now seeing Sweden's situation as increasingly dire, Gustav IV Adolf decided to revoke the ceasefire with France, forge a new treaty of alliance with the United Kingdom and resume the Franco-Swedish war.

Meanwhile, Danish commercial circles had pressured Crown Prince Frederik to resist British attempts to blockade French ports, which raised fears in London that Denmark's fleet might fall into French hands and be used against the British. Consequently, on September 2, 1807, the United Kingdom launched another attack on Copenhagen. During the six-week bombardment, a significant part of the city was destroyed, and the British departed with approximately 160 Danish ships.

Crown Prince Frederik now joined Napoleon's Continental System and remained thereafter one of Napoleon's staunchest allies. The impact of this decision on Denmark was negative from the outset. With Danish ports subjected to the British

The British bombardment of Copenhagen in 1807 destroyed a significant part of the city.

blockade, its once lucrative international trade dwindled. By 1813, the country faced bankruptcy due to soaring inflation, and famine erupted in Denmark's West Indian colonies, which had been reliant on grain imports, now disrupted by the blockade.

From the Swedish point of view, Denmark's alignment with Napoleon meant that Sweden and Portugal were the sole remaining British allies on the European continent, making war almost inevitable.

In February 1808, Tsar Alexander I dispatched his forces to Finland, citing Gustav IV Adolf's alliance with the United Kingdom as a justification. By the end of 1808, Russian troops had conquered most of Finland and were already harassing the Swedish coastline. Meanwhile, Crown Prince Frederik, who in March 1808 had become King Frederick VI of Denmark, hoped to capitalize on the situation and recapture

Skåne from Sweden with the assistance of French and Spanish forces. This plan was only thwarted when a rebellion broke out among the Spanish soldiers over Napoleon's handling of the Spanish succession question.

Dissatisfaction with Gustav IV Adolf deepened in Sweden, ultimately leading to his arrest and forced abdication on March 13, 1809. His uncle, Charles XIII (1748–1818), was crowned the new king, and a new constitution was adopted in the same year, formally ending absolutist rule and putting in place a power-sharing arrangement between Sweden's four-estate *Riksdag* and the king. The king retained legislative power, the right to veto laws, the authority to appoint ministers and control over foreign policy, while the parliament gained the right to legislate, impose taxes and reject the king's proposals. However, the constitution remained highly undemocratic, representing only about 7 percent of the Swedish population, and the old aristocracy continued to play the main role in the country's governance.

The primary goal of those who deposed Gustav IV Adolf had been to make peace with Russia. This was achieved in September 1809 with the Treaty of Fredrikshamn (also known as the Treaty of Hamina), under which Sweden relinquished to Russia a third of its territory: Finland, the Åland Islands and part of northern Sweden. These areas subsequently became the Grand Duchy of Finland, an autonomous part of the Russian Empire. There, Tsar Alexander I assumed the supreme authority, but left in place the absolutist system established by Gustav III, which was ratified by the Finnish Diet in Porvoo in 1809. The everyday governance of the Grand Duchy was overseen by a Senate, consisting of influential nobles of Swedish descent, who in turn were subordinated to a Russian governor-general.

As a result of the Fredrikshamn peace treaty, Sweden joined Napoleon's Continental System. The following year, an official peace treaty was signed with Denmark. However, neither Denmark nor Sweden had a reason to be satisfied with these treaties. Many in Sweden harbored hopes of reclaiming Finland, while Frederick VI, who was a claimant to the Swedish throne, dreamed of a new Nordic union under his leadership. The latter's ambitions were dashed in 1810, when former French marshal Jean-Baptiste Bernadotte (1763–1844), who in Sweden became known as Karl Johan (Charles John), was appointed the crown prince of childless Charles XIII.

Karl Johan saw an opportunity to compensate for the loss of Finland by conquering Norway, so when the alliance between France and Russia dissolved in 1812, Sweden joined forces with Russia, the United Kingdom and Austria in a new coalition against Napoleon. Swedish forces participated in the Battle of Leipzig in October 1813, where Napoleon suffered a decisive defeat.

Denmark's Frederick VI, for his part, remained loyal to France, which was proved to have been a grave policy mistake when Karl Johan moved Swedish troops to Holstein, threatening to attack Jutland. Diplomatically isolated, Frederick VI did not dare to confront Sweden and instead preferred to sign a peace treaty in Kiel on January 14, 1814. Under the Treaty of Kiel, Norway was ceded to the Swedish King, but Denmark retained control over Norway's North Atlantic tribute lands:

the Faroe Islands, Iceland and Greenland. This marked the end of more than 400 years of Danish rule in Norway.

For Sweden, however, Norway was far from an unproblematic acquisition. The Norwegian national awakening, which had begun in the late eighteenth century, intensified into a protest movement when Norway was severely impacted by the British blockade during the war. Although these protests primarily targeted Britain, King Frederick VI had expressed concerns over them early on and, in May 1813, appointed Crown Prince Christian Frederik (1786–1848) as his viceroy to ensure that Norway remained under Danish control.

When the Treaty of Kiel was signed, Christian Frederik initially sought to declare Norway independent and establish himself as its absolutist monarch. However, on February 19,

In February 1814, an assembly of Norwegian delegates convened at Eidsvoll and drafted a remarkably liberal constitution, which remains in force today.

1814, a constitutional assembly was called to convene at Eidsvoll, north of Christiania (now Oslo). Meeting for the first time on April 4, this assembly of delegates from across Norway and various social classes drafted a remarkably liberal constitution, which was signed on May 17. On the same day, the assembly elected Christian Frederik as the king of Norway.

The 1814 Norwegian constitution, which remains in force to this day, established a limited and hereditary monarchy, granting the king the right to appoint ministers, initiate legislation, veto bills and conduct foreign policy. It also created the institution of the parliament (*Storting*), with legislative authority, the power to levy taxes and the ability to override the king's veto. This new parliament was to represent approximately 12 percent of the Norwegian population, but the constitution stipulated that two-thirds of its members must come from rural areas.

The day after the new constitution was adopted, Christian Frederik, who had hoped for foreign support for Norwegian independence, learned that no assistance could be expected either from the United Kingdom or from Denmark. Crown Prince Karl Johan, for his part, responded by dispatching his troops to Norway at the end of July. His goal, however, was not military conquest, but to get rid of Christian Frederik and negotiate with Norwegian representatives directly. On August 14, a peace treaty was signed in Moss, where Karl Johan accepted the legitimacy of the Eidsvoll Constitution, and Christian Frederik agreed to abdicate and leave the country.

In October, the *Storting* convened, and by November 4 the Eidsvoll Constitution had been sufficiently modified to be acceptable to Sweden. Charles XIII was elected king of Norway, and in early 1815 the *Riksakten*, or Act of Union, gave a legal form to the personal union between Norway and Sweden. While Norway retained full autonomy in domestic politics, Sweden and the king dominated foreign policy.

For Sweden, the union with Norway could not quite make up for the loss of Finland, formerly the eastern third of the Swedish state. Yet by declaring Sweden a satisfied power and concluding an alliance with Russia against a possible French attack (the so-called "policy of 1812"), Crown Prince Karl Johan now turned the focus of Swedish foreign policy away from the east and toward the west.

The Napoleonic Wars had highlighted the essential vulnerability of the Scandinavian kingdoms and the importance of careful maneuvering between the interests of great powers. The opportunistic foreign policy choices of Gustav IV Adolf and Frederick VI had proved remarkably detrimental to their respective countries: Gustav IV Adolf's turn against Napoleon had led to the loss of Finland to Russia, while Frederick VI's steadfast alliance with Napoleon after 1812 resulted in the loss of Norway to Sweden. As relatively small states, Sweden and Denmark thus had strong incentives to stay out of further military adventures. In Sweden's case, this commenced a tradition of neutrality and non-alignment that remained in effect for the following two hundred years.

THE BERNADOTTE DYNASTY

Frenchman Jean-Baptiste Bernadotte, who in 1810 was invited to Sweden to serve as crown prince and then as king, was in some ways a surprising choice for the throne, as he had commanded French troops in battle against the Swedish army in Pomerania early in the war. Later, during his reign as king of Sweden (as Charles XIV John) and king of Norway (as Charles III John), from 1818 to 1844, he became a Lutheran but did not learn Swedish or Norwegian.

Charles John was initially popular in Sweden, not least because he had successfully extricated Sweden from the Napoleonic Wars and gained some form of compensation for the loss of Finland. However, by the 1840s, his autocratic style of rule had come under increasingly strong criticism. His son, Oscar I (1799–1859), who ruled from 1844 to 1859, even came into conflict with his father during his time as the viceroy of Norway (1824–33), as Charles XIV John suspected his son of conspiring against him, together with the independence-minded politicians in the Norwegian *Storting*. However, when Oscar I ascended the throne, it became evident that his liberalism was rather cautious. He promoted press freedom and granted more rights to Norway, but he refrained from reforming the outdated 1809 constitution.

The Bernadotte dynasty still occupies the Swedish throne today, as the monarchy has continued to adapt and evolve with the times. King Gustav V (1858–1950), who ruled Sweden through both world wars, came into sharp conflict with the parliament in 1914, but he subsequently adopted a less activist stance. The Swedish monarchs that followed him, such as the present king, Carl XVI Gustaf (1946–), have had a mostly ceremonial role.

11

ROMANTIC NATIONALISM, LIBERALISM AND SCANDINAVIANISM

THE DECADES OF THE EARLY and mid-nineteenth century were undoubtedly a time of great change in Western political and intellectual history. New modernizing ideologies that had been boosted by the French Revolution and the Napoleonic Wars—especially liberalism and romantic nationalism—exercised significant influence across Europe, undermining the traditional authority of the monarchy and the church, and promoting an essentially secular view of the world. Eventually, this gradual breakthrough of ideas about civil rights, popular sovereignty and nationalism would culminate in the collapse of several multinational European empires during the end stage and aftermath of World War I.

In the Nordic region, the nations that lacked independent statehood—Iceland, Finland and Norway—developed grassroots movements that embraced German philosopher Johann Gottfried Herder's ideas about the unique value of every nation, which eventually turned into political liberation movements aiming for national independence. In the ancient kingdoms of Sweden and Denmark, romantic nationalism also had a significant cultural impact, but its political influence was less important, and the Enlightenment traditions inherited from the eighteenth century remained stronger.

At the same time, the political environment was not particularly welcoming for new ideas of nationalism and liberalism. The decades after the Napoleonic Wars were a period of conservative restoration, with European empires attempting a return to some form of a stable international system. Nevertheless, the influence of the new ideas proved to be impossible to rein in, even in states such as Denmark, which still had an absolutist system of governance.

After its series of foreign policy failures during the Napoleonic Wars, Denmark faced severe economic repercussions, but remained a conservative ancien régime, even after King Frederick VI was succeeded by his cousin Christian VIII (1786–1848) in 1839. Yet, perhaps paradoxically, the first half of the nineteenth century also marked one of its cultural peaks. Renowned figures in literature and philosophy, such as Hans Christian Andersen (1805–75), Søren Kierkegaard (1813–55), Nikolai Frederik Severin Grundtvig (1783–1872) and Adam Oehlenschläger (1779–1850), and many famous artists, left indelible marks not only on Danish culture but on European culture at large. This earned the era the title of the Danish Golden Age. Oehlenschläger's romantic tragedies, which drew inspiration from Scandinavian history and Old Norse mythology, marked the advent of national romanticism, the literary and artistic style associated with romantic nationalism, in the

Nordic region more broadly, and Grundtvig—a clergyman, historian, philologist and poet—contributed significantly to the Danish national awakening with his multifaceted endeavors that also influenced the rest of Scandinavia.

This statue of prolific Danish author Hans Christian Andersen stands in the Rosenborg Castle Gardens in Copenhagen, Denmark.

National romanticism also found a fertile ground in Sweden, still reeling from the 1809 loss of Finland and looking for new sources of national pride. This period saw the establishment of numerous associations dedicated to the study of Swedish language, history and culture. Notably, the Geatish Society (Götiska Förbundet), founded in 1811, was meant to uplift the moral character of the Swedish nation by promoting interest in Vikings and Norse mythology. Poets such as Erik Gustaf Geijer (1783–1847) and Esaias Tegnér (1782–1846) incorporated motifs from *The Poetic Edda* (an Icelandic collection of heroic and mythological poems composed between 800 and 1100 CE) and medieval Icelandic romances into their works, and Geijer's famous poems "Odalbonden" and "Vikingen" offered two contrasting portrayals of Swedish identity, with the former depicting an indigenous Swedish farmer rooted in ancestral lands, and the latter an adventurous youth driven by a thirst for exploration. Similar themes permeated Swedish national-romantic art and music.

The Norwegian national awakening, more aligned with Herder's original vision, paralleled the national awakening of other stateless European nationalities. Some of the most famous figures of the Norwegian national movement—such as Peter Christen Asbjørnsen (1812–85), Jørgen Moe (1813–82) and Ivar Aasen (1813–96)—focused on collecting folklore, educating the peasantry and cultivating an identity rooted in a strong national language and culture. The urban elites in Norway were primarily Danish-speaking, which created a readily apparent distinction between them and the lower classes, and steered the national movement to associate true Norwegianness with the rural populace. Furthermore, unlike in Denmark, Norwegian farmers had always enjoyed personal freedom, which was regarded as a source of national pride. In general, even though the Norwegian national awakening took place under Swedish rule, it was primarily directed against Danish influence.

Icelandic nationalism first emerged in student circles at the University of Copenhagen in the 1830s. Young scholars and poets, such as Jónas Hallgrímsson (1807–45), interpreted the catastrophic events that had befallen Iceland in the 1780s as the consequence of centuries-long colonial oppression, and a sign of spiritual and material decline after the end of Iceland's medieval era of freedom. The inability of the Danish government to react adequately to the 1783 volcanic eruption was viewed as merely the latest example of how a distant central authority could not handle issues that a local and more flexible government would be able to address better. An important initial goal of the movement was the restoration of the *Alþingi* (the Icelandic assembly), which was achieved in 1845.

Finland, which had been transferred to Russia in 1809, also developed a distinctive national movement. Indeed, its new status as an autonomous great duchy in the Russian Empire greatly aided the birth of Finnish nationalism. Cut off from the Swedish motherland, but retaining their high social status, the liberal-minded part of Finland's Swedish-speaking intelligentsia established the Fennoman movement in the 1820s, which focused on the promotion of Finnish language, culture and education, not just among the Finnish-speaking peasants but also among the intellectuals themselves. The Fennomans embraced Finnish folklore, nature and language as symbols of national pride and unity, with artists, writers and musicians drawing inspiration from epic poetry, such as Elias Lönnrot's (1802–84) *Kalevala*, and the Finnish landscape to create works that reflected the unique Finnish spirit. In this, they were initially encouraged by the Russian state, which had a natural interest in loosening the cultural and political ties between Finland and Sweden.

For most of this time, romantic nationalism was closely allied and intertwined with liberalism. It was only in the final decades of the nineteenth century that a more conservative nationalist ideology would gain prominence, co-opted by the traditional conservative elites. Until then, liberal ideas helped to promote national liberation and political modernization alike.

During Frederick VI's reign, Denmark had reverted to a more absolutist stance: political opposition was banned, and a limited freedom of the press was allowed only in the mid-1830s. Similarly, in Sweden, Crown Prince Karl Johan, who in 1818 became King Charles XIV John, wielded strong personal power within the bounds of the authoritarian constitution of 1809. Only in Norway was his power curbed by the *Storting*, which was liberal-minded—one example of this was its abolishment of noble privileges in 1821. Consequently, there was no need in Norway for a separate grassroots liberal movement, as the *Storting* itself acted as one.

But even in the parts of the region governed in a more authoritarian fashion, liberal ideas continued to exercise influence. In Denmark, the spread of liberalism in the 1830s was largely facilitated by the advisory representative bodies that had been established as a result of the Duchy of Holstein's inclusion in the German Confederation, after the Congress of Vienna (1814–15). This had come with an obligation to institute some form of popular political representation. In 1831, similar representative bodies were established in Schleswig, Jutland and Iceland, serving as forums for the national liberal opposition. Under King Christian VIII, this opposition became more vocal, with critical newspapers prompting the king to distribute loyalist propaganda to counter them.

Christian VIII's hesitant policy in Schleswig and Holstein was subjected to particular criticism.

In 1848, a series of national liberal revolutionary attempts took place in France, Italy, Austria and elsewhere, aimed at challenging the aristocratic social order. These events also deeply affected Denmark, where Christian VIII had recently died. Threatened by uprisings in Schleswig and Holstein, and as mass protest meetings in Copenhagen demanded universal suffrage and liberal government, the new king, Frederick VII (1808–63), had to concede to reforms. In March, a new government that included members of the national liberal opposition took office, and elections for a national constituent assembly were announced. On June 5, 1849, a new Danish constitution was adopted, establishing a bicameral parliament and granting voting rights to all male property owners over the age of thirty. Around the same time, slavery was officially abolished in the Danish West Indies. The era of absolutism had finally ended in Denmark.

The duchies nevertheless remained problematic, as Schleswig and Holstein saw the emergence of two nationalist factions, one emphasizing the duchies' autonomous identity, and the other sympathetic to the idea of a united Germany. The latter movement gained the upper hand, and from 1848 to 1851, the duchies revolted against Danish central authority, demanding unification with Germany. Prussia attempted to use this opportunity to annex Holstein and Lauenburg, resulting in the so-called Three Years' War from 1848 to 1850. After major battles involving thousands of soldiers, the war ended with a Danish victory, but also contributed to Denmark's transformation into a constitutional monarchy in 1849.

Subsequently, the status quo persisted until a new escalation in the 1860s, when the duchies' German-speaking secessionist movement once again gained Prussian support. In response, Danish nationalists began demanding the full incorporation of Schleswig into Denmark, hoping for military assistance from Sweden and Norway in the event of war. In 1863, Denmark's national liberal government indeed fully incorporated Schleswig into the Danish state, and in January 1864, Prussian and Austrian forces attacked Denmark. No major power came to Denmark's aid, and the hoped-for support from Sweden and Norway did not materialize. Denmark was forced to sign a peace treaty, losing all of Holstein and Lauenburg, and almost all of Schleswig, to Prussia.

This painting of the First Schleswig War (1864) is by Wilhelm Camphausen, an artist who accompanied the Prussian forces during the conflict and painted several scenes of the fighting.

For the Danes, the defeat meant significant national humiliation and a continuation of the once-great Danish kingdom's disintegration, a process that had begun with the seventeenth-century territorial losses to Sweden. After 1864, something of a generational shift also occurred in the Danish liberal movement: those born after 1840 accused the earlier "national liberals" of having failed to prevent wars and the loss of Schleswig. On the back of this failure, Denmark adopted a new, more conservative constitution in 1866, which integrated Iceland as a regular part of the Danish state in 1871. At the same time, the defeat had fostered a greater sense of national unity and a determination to compensate for the defeat in the duchies with internal development. Denmark's economy began to recover, largely thanks to the impact of liberal ideas on economic and trade policy.

The same ideas had also quickly reached Sweden, yet progress was impeded by the fact that the middle classes who supported them were underrepresented in political life. Sweden's traditional four-estate parliament did not pay heed to the differing political views within each estate, but instead reflected the medieval mindset, according to which each person was to remain in their divinely ordained place in society and social mobility was discouraged. Liberals began pressuring for the abolition of Sweden's old-fashioned parliament in the early nineteenth century, demanding one modeled after the British system, with two chambers and voting rights for each member. In the 1830s, Sweden also saw the emergence of a liberal press, with influential newspapers such as *Aftonbladet* contributing to the dissemination of liberal ideas.

News of the attempted revolutions of 1848 elsewhere in Europe also received a response in Sweden, and riots took place in Stockholm in support of liberal reforms, including to parliament, resulting in the deaths of around thirty people. However, the reforms did not materialize. It was only in 1866 that a new parliamentary law replaced Sweden's old four-estate parliament with a bicameral British-style parliament. Even after that, the power of conservative elites mostly remained intact, due to the very limited suffrage that covered only 21 percent of all adult men over the age of twenty-one.

A particularly Scandinavian current of thought in the nineteenth century was the so-called Scandinavianist movement. Its ideology rested on the ideas that a nation's destiny inevitably steered it toward the establishment of a sovereign state, and that the nation was to be defined in terms of shared language and culture. The relative similarity of Scandinavian languages and cultures suggested that the whole of Scandinavia should eventually be united into a single state. Indeed, according to this thinking, Scandinavia constituted a potential great power in the waiting, one that could, in future, be capable of thwarting external threats from other great powers, notably Russia and Germany.

As Sweden's policy of 1812 discouraged further adventurism in the east, the foreign policy side of Swedish liberal nationalism was quite inclined to develop in the pan-Scandinavian direction. Especially among university students, early organisations such as the Geatish Society gave way in the 1840s to a broader Scandinavianist movement, championed by cultural figures such as Esaias Tegnér and Adam Oehlenschläger.

Even more significantly, the new Swedish-Norwegian monarch, Oscar I's eldest son, Charles XV (1826–72) (in Sweden) or Charles IV (in Norway), who ascended the throne in 1859, was a supporter of Scandinavianism. More liberal than his predecessor, he implemented legal reforms, including Sweden's criminal law reform in 1864, and finally abolished Sweden's four-estates parliament in 1866. Charles XV was also a friend of Frederick VII, and allegedly promised Swedish and Norwegian military assistance in case of another war with Prussia.

This, however, set the scene for disappointment when Swedish and Norwegian aid during the 1864 war over Schleswig and Holstein did not materialize. Having failed this test, Scandinavianism declined as a political idea but remained relevant in the sphere of culture, where it stood as a historical precedent for many subsequent initiatives at Nordic cooperation.

HANS CHRISTIAN ANDERSEN

Hans Christian Andersen (1805–75), born on April 2, 1805, in Odense, Denmark, is one of the most renowned authors of fairy tales in the world and a major cultural figure of nineteenth-century Denmark. Andersen's early life was marked by poverty and hardship. His father died when Andersen was eleven, leaving Andersen's mother, a washerwoman, to support the family. Nevertheless, Andersen showed a keen interest in literature and theater from a young age, and at fourteen moved to Copenhagen with aspirations of becoming an actor or singer.

After initial struggles, he gained the patronage of Jonas Collin, director of the Royal Danish Theatre, who helped him receive a proper education. Andersen became a prolific writer of poetry, plays, travelogues and novels, yet he is best remembered for his fairy tales. His first collection of these, published in 1835, included such stories as "The Tinderbox," "Little Claus and Big Claus" and "The Princess and the Pea," showcasing Andersen's unique ability to blend fantasy with real-life lessons, in simple, imaginative plots that have been appreciated by children and adults alike. The characters often include underdogs and outcasts who overcome adversity, possibly reflecting Andersen's own experiences of feeling like an outsider. Over the years, Andersen wrote many more beloved tales, including "The Little Mermaid," "The Ugly Duckling" and "The Emperor's New Clothes."

Andersen traveled extensively throughout Europe, which broadened his perspective and influenced his writing. He died on August 4, 1875, in Copenhagen. Today, his fairy tales have been translated into more than 125 languages.

12

ECONOMIC AND SOCIAL MODERNIZATION: LATE 1800s–EARLY 1900s

ONE WAY OF CONCEPTUALIZING nineteenth-century European history would be as a time shaped by two revolutions: the Industrial Revolution and the French Revolution. The spread of liberal democracy and liberal capitalism did not always coincide, but the relevant ideas complemented each other, merging into a broad process of economic and societal modernization. The old social order based on estates, and wealth based on ownership of land—both contested in the eighteenth century—now gave way to a new order dominated by the middle class, liberal ideas and profits derived from commerce and industry.

The Industrial Revolution, which in some European countries had already begun in the eighteenth century, was a particularly powerful phenomenon, exerting pressure on the whole continent. To avoid being outcompeted, all European states were strongly incentivized to attract investment in their industry and commerce. Success or failure had important consequences: the better a country could industrialize, the greater its chances at economic, political and even military domination of others. Falling behind, on the other hand, meant all-round weakening, and possibly even loss of independence and absorption by other states. The countries most under threat were therefore those that could not industrialize quickly enough.

Scandinavia was a latecomer, but not extremely so, to the Industrial Revolution. It arrived around the mid-nineteenth century and came to full force in the 1870s. Once established, it brought rapid economic development and far-reaching changes in Scandinavian societies. The economy came to be dominated by industrial production, enriching the nascent middle class and creating a working class, which became first economically, and then politically, influential. The struggle for women's rights, parliamentary reform and extension of suffrage intensified. This inevitably meant sharp conflicts of interest with the outnumbered conservative elites. At the same time, mass emigration provided an alternative outlet for economic and political discontent.

Thanks to superior natural resources, the union of Sweden and Norway held a competitive industrial edge over Denmark, which remained predominantly agricultural long into the twentieth century. Sweden and Norway could supply large quantities of timber and iron ore, which were crucial raw materials for both export and domestic manufacturing. The main wood-producing regions were in northern Sweden (Ådalen; the Sundsvall area) and southern Norway (Skien; Drammen). Beginning in the mid-nineteenth century, much of this wood was turned into cellulose, of which Sweden had become the world's largest exporter by the beginning of World War I.

Sweden also benefited from improved production methods for metals, as iron ore could now be turned into higher-quality steel without dependence on charcoal. In the 1890s, the metal industry began to expand in northern Sweden (Gällivare; Kiruna), and was especially boosted by the construction of the railway to the Norwegian port of Narvik in 1902. Toward the end of the nineteenth century, Sweden's chemical industry also developed fast. And, thanks to its vast hydro-power resources, Sweden–Norway was one of the earliest European states—around 1890—to become a major producer and user of electricity.

Denmark, too, rapidly industrialized from the 1870s onward. Its exports increased, and the entire country was covered by a railway network. The population of Copenhagen, which in 1800 had been 100,000, grew to 500,000 by 1900. In Iceland and the Faroe Islands, where industrialization was linked to the development of industrial fishing, urbanization had an even more significant impact. In 1880, only 5 percent of Icelanders had lived in urban settlements, but this figure had risen to 32 percent by 1910.

On a broader cultural level, the Industrial Revolution brought with it new faith in modern technology and economic development, which some even hoped could lead to the resolution of social problems. Signs of progress were indeed evident. Economic growth created jobs, and new communication and transportation opportunities connected places and people in unprecedented ways. The nineteenth century was a golden age for inventions and inventors, with the most prominent Scandinavian example being the Swedish inventor of dynamite, Alfred Nobel (1833–96).

Characteristic of this optimism were large industrial exhibitions that showcased new technical marvels to a broader public. The first industrial exhibition in Stockholm took place in 1866, with participation from Scandinavian countries and the Russian Empire. Plans for the next exhibition began immediately but came to fruition only in 1897. The Great Stockholm Exhibition, when it finally took place, was extremely popular.

The Machine Hall was one of many spectacular buildings erected for the Great Stockholm Exhibition of 1897.

Economic growth led to people having more leisure time, which meant that for the first time in history, significant sections of society could take vacations in the countryside or by the sea. Social mobility also became much more easily achievable. A notably successful example was J.C. (Jacob Christian) Jacobsen (1811–87), who founded the Carlsberg brewery and became one of the wealthiest men of his time. He served in the Copenhagen city council and the Danish parliament, established the Carlsberg Foundation to support art and science, and even financed the reconstruction of Frederiksborg Castle—the Danish royal palace—after it burnt down in 1859.

New middle-class lifestyles and urbanization would have far-reaching effects on family life. In urban settings, the role of women changed: while men worked outside the home, women's area of responsibility was increasingly limited to household chores. But since few goods (such as grains, vegetables, fruit, meat, milk and eggs) were produced at home anymore, the status of women's work declined. Upper-middle-class women, whose household chores were done by servants, often engaged in voluntary charity and social work to escape forced idleness and have something of a career.

Especially among middle-class men, membership in clubs and voluntary associations became common. Most of these clubs and associations were connected with the so-called folk movements. One of these was the temperance movement—a societal reaction to the industrialized production, and therefore increased consumption, of alcohol, which had developed into a broad societal problem. The temperance movement was, in turn, close to the Pietistic revival movement, which, in a rapidly secularizing world, urged people toward religiosity. But there were also educational societies, workers' societies, farmers' cooperative societies and the emerging women's movement.

The women's movement in Scandinavia began in the 1830s with demands for women's equality with men before the law. In Europe women still lacked citizenship, legal independence and free access to the labor market and education. The movement followed a similar pattern to other grassroots movements, beginning with spontaneous activism, followed by focused efforts and eventually leading to the establishment of organizations advocating for political rights, such as the Danish Women's Society, founded in 1871, and the Fredrika Bremer Association in Sweden, founded in 1884. Some early important successes, such as inheritance rights and economic independence for women, were achieved in Denmark in 1857 and in Sweden in 1858.

Fredrika Bremer was a popular novelist and a pioneer of the women's movement in Sweden.

However, the main reasons behind the advancement of women's rights were not moral or legal, but economic. The steps taken to improve women's situation helped to make them more productive members of the workforce and prevented them from becoming a burden on society—for instance, in the event of losing a breadwinning spouse. By the mid-nineteenth century, women had gained inheritance rights and economic freedom, but they were still not allowed to choose their own husbands. The first two reforms directly served the needs of the economy; the last one did not.

Another crucial grassroots movement that emerged in the nineteenth century was the labor movement, which rose to prominence as a consequence of the Industrial Revolution. Initially with very limited rights and bargaining power, workers organized themselves into trade unions to better represent their interests. In its earliest phase, in the 1850s and 1860s, the labor movement was essentially liberal in nature, focusing on uplifting workers' education and moral standards, and providing them with economic assistance, but in the 1870s, more radical socialist ideas began to gain traction. Far more militant in pressing workers' demands than the liberals, the social democrats rapidly expanded their influence and took over many trade unions. Their central aim was to assert workers' right to strike. By the end of the decade, some early instances of labor unrest had indeed taken place, such as Sweden's 1879 Sundsvall strike, with some five thousand participants. But success was rare, and many workers remained wary of radical political affiliations.

In 1871, the first Scandinavian social-democratic party, the

NORDIC MODERNISM

The changes in Nordic societies in the last decades of the nineteenth century and the beginning of the twentieth century found a strong response in the innovative and experimental work of Scandinavian writers, composers and artists. Influenced by European modernism more generally, the Scandinavian figures nevertheless retained a uniquely Nordic voice.

The Swedish playwright, novelist, poet and essayist August Strindberg (1849–1912) became internationally renowned for his psychologically and existentially charged works, often rooted in personal experience. Similarly, the Norwegian playwright Henrik Ibsen (1828–1906), novelist Knut Hamsun (1859–1952) and historical novelist Sigrid Undset (1882–1949) were distinguished by their nuanced portrayals of societal pressures, personal isolation and alienation in a modernizing world.

The Norwegian Edvard Grieg (1843–1907), a leading Romantic composer who blended Norwegian folk music with rich harmonic textures, gave way in the late nineteenth century to late Romantic composers such as the Finn Jean Sibelius (1865–1957), whose symphonies, imbued with natural and folk influences, gave expression to a strong sense of Finnish nationalism.

The visual art of the period also mirrored broad cultural shifts around national identity, existentialism and tensions between modernity and tradition. Norwegian painter Edvard Munch (1863–1944), renowned for *The Scream*, created emotionally charged, symbolic works that explored themes of anxiety, alienation and the psychological struggles of modern individuals. Danish painter Vilhelm Hammershøi (1864–1916), in contrast, is known for his quiet, introspective depictions of urban and indoor settings, characterized by emotional restraint and melancholy. Finnish artist Akseli Gallén-Kallela (1865–1931) blended symbolism with national romanticism, drawing on Finnish folklore and mythology, much as Sibelius did with his music.

International Labour Association of Denmark, was founded under the leadership of Louis Pio (1841–94), drawing inspiration from the German Social Democratic Party. However, it faced significant opposition from the Danish state; in 1877, Pio was presented with a one-way ticket to America. A decade later, social-democratic parties were founded in Norway, in 1887, and in Sweden, in 1889. The program of the latter, authored by Hjalmar Branting (1860– 1925), outlined radical political demands such as universal suffrage, an eight-hour workday, free education and the abolition of the military and the state church.

Soon, however, internal divisions appeared in left-wing politics. The First International, a union of socialist workers' organizations that had been established under the guidance of Marx and Engels in 1864, was dissolved in 1876, due to tensions between social democrats and anarchists. Subsequently, the social democrats themselves split into revolutionary and revisionist wings. This gap became increasingly insurmountable in Scandinavia as well.

In 1898–99, trade union federations were established in Denmark, Sweden and Norway, and the labor movement had become a significant societal and political force by the turn of the century. Facing the threat of strikes, employers were often compelled to conclude collective wage agreements and formed their own organizations in response. At the same time, some social democrats, such as Sweden's Hjalmar Branting, emerged as influential parliamentarians.

Yet another popular movement of sorts was the emigration movement. Between 1830 and 1930, almost three million

Scandinavians—including 200,000 Danes, 800,000 Norwegians and 1.3 million Swedes—emigrated, mainly to North America. Of course, the Scandinavian countries were not exceptional in this regard. Between 1800 and 1914, 85 percent of Europe's population migrated somewhere, with 15 percent moving abroad and 70 percent moving from rural areas to cities.

To a significant extent, migration was driven by overpopulation: between 1800 and 1914, the population of Scandinavia had tripled, driven by factors that Swedish poet Esaias Tegnér succinctly characterized as "peace, vaccine, and potatoes." Apart from the two Schleswig wars, after 1814 there was indeed a long period of peace in Scandinavia, meaning that young men were not drafted into wars and more children were born. Additionally, vaccination against smallpox became widespread in the nineteenth century, and improved medical education, hygiene and hospitals played a role in reducing mortality further. The introduction of potatoes as a dominant crop meant that while famines still occurred, widespread famine became uncommon. As a result, birth rates remained high, but mortality, especially infant mortality, decreased significantly.

In an insufficiently industrialized region, population growth had negative consequences. The number of available jobs could not be dynamically increased, as agricultural expansion was limited by available farmland. At the same time, the increase in heirs caused many farms to be divided up into small parcels that could not feed a family, adding to rural poverty. But these were not the only causes of emigration.

Some members of religious communities—such as Pietists, Methodists, Baptists and Mormons—left due to the repressive state church. Political reasons, such as the overly rigid social hierarchy and lack of democracy, also played a role, as did the risk of conscription into the army.

"Do not travel to America": a Swedish anti-emigration sign.

The reasons that attracted emigrants to various destinations included economic opportunities, such as cheaper cost of living or better-paying jobs; religious freedom; more democratic and open societies; the existence of immigrant communities of the same origin; propaganda in newspapers and books—and even just the chance to start over after some personal misfortune.

The first nineteenth-century emigrant groups from Scandinavia were religious communities. In 1825, fifty-three Norwegian Quakers from Stavanger arrived in New York state and then settled in Illinois, where Swedish pastor Erik Jansson (1808–50) and his followers founded Bishop Hill in 1846. Initially, whole families often emigrated together, hoping to establish a farm and start a new life. But this changed after emigration intensified in the 1870s, with the beginning of regular transoceanic transportation. By the 1880s, most emigrants were traveling alone or in small, unrelated groups. After arrival, they typically settled in urban areas, looking for jobs, rather than establishing new rural communities.

In the end, migration from Scandinavia was a multifaceted phenomenon. It served as a relief valve for overpopulation, potentially averting political tensions and economic destitution at home. However, emigration also caused concerns about the future of the nation. Although emigrants did not necessarily sever ties with their homelands, and many returned with ideas or capital that were put to use in Scandinavia, it was people of working age who were most likely to leave. Economic downturns, such as the one that hit Scandinavia in the 1860s, correlated with the rise in emigration, particularly as rapid economic growth occurred in postbellum America. In the end, the onset of World War I decreased emigration significantly, and by the 1920s, mass emigration from Scandinavia had come to an end.

EMIGRATION AND NORDIC IDENTITY ABROAD

Depending on where emigrants ended up, some of them assimilated almost immediately, while others retained their language for several generations. This was especially the case in rural communities, where ethnic churches played an important role in preserving the Scandinavian identity. Some of these communities were very homogeneous, consisting of families from the same parish or village who had emigrated together. In places such as Porter, Indiana, children continued to be educated in their parents' native languages well into the interwar period.

In urban settings such as Chicago, home to a large Swedish community, secular organizations—including sport or theater societies, ethnic trade unions, clubs and local history societies—played a significant role as well.

Also important for preserving ethnic identity was access to journalism and literature in the heritage language. Starting with the newspaper *Skandinavia* in New York in 1847, hundreds of Scandinavian-language newspapers were eventually established in the United States, catering to various political and religious views. Most of these were not published in English until the 1920s, and many found readers in other, non-local, Scandinavian-speaking communities, fostering a broad Scandinavian identity in emigration. Emigrant literature, often dealing with the emigration experience, also emerged, with notable authors including the Swede Ernst Skarstedt (1857–1929), the Norwegian Ole Edvart Rølvaag (1876–1931) and the Dane Sophus Keith Winther (1893–1983).

Over time and across generations, Scandinavian identity tended to fade, but it saw a resurgence in the post–World War II decades, with people increasingly embracing hybrid identities such as Danish American or Swedish American. Today, many communities and individuals in the United States and elsewhere retain a strong degree of interest in their Scandinavian past.

13

MODERN PARLIAMENTARISM AND THE END OF THE SWEDISH–NORWEGIAN UNION

IN THE FINAL DECADES OF THE nineteenth century and in the early twentieth century, Scandinavia experienced even sharper conflicts between popular demands for increased democratic representation, on the one hand, and outdated political structures that were unwilling or unable to accommodate them, on the other. Again, these conflicts were not unique to Scandinavia: the feasibility and desirability of democracy was being debated throughout Europe, with significant disagreements on key questions, such as whether the government should be appointed by the parliament or by the head of state, and who should be allowed to vote in elections. Initially, the main disagreements were between liberals and conservatives, but soon the social democrats joined the discussion as well.

In Denmark, the first modern political parties—conservative Højre and liberal Venstre—emerged in the 1870s, with the

Social Democrats added in 1876. Venstre's program included demands for a more democratic constitution and government accountability to parliament, following the Norwegian example. These aspirations, however, had a formidable enemy in King Christian IX (1818–1906), who ascended to the throne in 1863. Having suffered a blow to his reputation because of the Danish defeat in the Second Schleswig War, Christian IX was made even more unpopular by his determination to rein in liberalization with his support for the longstanding (1875–94), conservative cabinet of Prime Minister Jacob Brønnum Scavenius Estrup (1825–1913), which opposed any political reforms.

However, in 1874, Christian IX reluctantly signed an agreement allowing Iceland a separate constitution, even as it remained part of Denmark, and, in 1901, he finally let Venstre's leader, Johan Henrik Deuntzer (1845–1918), form a government—a belated breakthrough for parliamentary democracy in Denmark. This was the first Danish government without conservatives. The Danish coalition governments in the run-up to World War I were primarily formed by the new Social Liberal Party (Radikale Venstre), which had split from Venstre in 1905, and Venstre itself.

Sweden, which likewise had a longstanding parliamentary tradition, did not experience a democratic breakthrough in the nineteenth century, but there was movement in the same direction. Cooperation between parliamentarians with similar political views had occurred even in the old, estates-based parliament. In the bicameral parliament established in 1866, group voting according to political views became more common, but only gradually led to the development of permanent parties. The strongest such group in the second (lower) chamber was Lantmannapartiet, representing the interests of small landowners. In the first chamber, parties did not emerge until the turn of the century, and many members of the parliament did not belong to a party at all, but rather grouped themselves around positions on various political issues in an ad hoc manner.

In 1876, the position of prime minister was established in Sweden, somewhat distancing the government from direct royal authority. However, neither the king nor the conservative governments that he appointed intended to tie the formation of government to having a majority in the second chamber. It was only during the 1905 union crisis that Prime Minister Karl Staaff (1860–1915) was given the opportunity to form the first parliamentary majority government in Sweden.

The Swedish monarch in the last decades of the nineteenth century and in the beginning of the twentieth was Oscar II (1829–1907), who ascended to the throne of Sweden–Norway after the death of his brother Charles XV in 1872. Conservative in his domestic politics, he asserted Swedish interests in the union with Norway, but nevertheless managed the Swedish–Norwegian political contradictions with sufficient tact to make possible the union's peaceful dissolution in 1905.

The Swedish–Norwegian union was always a comparatively mild example of imperialism. Even though Norway had been acquired through war, Sweden treated it relatively well, right from the outset. This was evident from the fact that Crown Prince Karl Johan of Sweden, despite holding

King Oscar II reigned over the united states of Sweden and Norway from 1872 until 1905, when he abdicated the Norwegian throne.

significant military superiority, negotiated the Moss agreement under very lenient terms and allowed the 1814 Norwegian constitution to remain in effect.

However, the union was far from devoid of conflict, as Sweden and Norway had diametrically different understandings of its basic nature. Sweden's interpretation rested on the political reality that Norway had been subjugated and therefore had to accept Swedish dominance. Norway's understanding instead emphasized the supremacy of its 1814 constitution, and the fact that the *Storting* never ratified the Treaty of Kiel. Not least because Norway's constitution was significantly more liberal than Sweden's, Norwegians tended to view Sweden's hegemonic aspirations as anachronistic and inappropriate.

Over time, Norwegian self-confidence was boosted by the general success of liberal ideas across Europe, as well as the country's own economic development. In the mid-nineteenth century, Norway had still been a predominantly pre-industrial society, with three quarters of its population engaged in farming and fishing. However, the following fifty years were a period of rapid industrial development, thanks to amply available hydropower resources. From 1801 to 1875, Norway's population grew by more than 100 percent, and many peasants moved from rural areas to cities or emigrated abroad.

Norway's liberal opposition remained closely tied to the *Storting*, which commenced annual meetings in the 1870s and quickly became a center of resistance against the government appointed by the king. In 1872, the *Storting* passed a law requiring government members to regularly report to the parliament, but it was vetoed by the king in support of government autonomy. When the liberal opposition won a majority in the 1882 elections, it adopted the law anyway, despite government opposition. This conflict over accountability gave rise to the first permanent Norwegian parties: Høyre, with its base among supporters of the government, and Venstre, representing the liberal opposition. Høyre believed that a governmental obligation to report to the *Storting* would violate the principle of separation of powers, while Venstre argued it would ensure greater attention to the will of the people.

In 1883–84, this matter went to court in Christiania (now Oslo), where the conservative government led by Christian August Selmer (1816–89) was found guilty of unconstitutional activities. Although King Oscar II considered military intervention to support the government, Selmer instead chose to resign. The cabinet that replaced it was led by former opposition leader Johan Sverdrup (1816–92). It had the support of the *Storting* and can be considered the first example of the parliamentary principle being followed in Scandinavia, predating that of Denmark in 1901. During Sverdrup's tenure, liberal reforms were implemented, including the expansion of voting rights.

Thanks to Norway's predominantly liberal politics, the attitude of the Swedish middle classes toward Norway's aspirations for independence was generally positive. Indeed, intellectuals such as Fredrika Bremer (1801–65), Adolf Hedin (1834–1905) and Ellen Key (1849–1926) tended to hold up the Norwegian people's quest for freedom as an example for Sweden. As a counterweight, there were some Norwegian conservative industrialists and academics who were in favor of preserving the union, but their influence was relatively small.

In the last decades of the century, the incompatibility of Swedish and Norwegian interests became increasingly evident on a range of issues related to foreign policy. Norway's economy relied more heavily on foreign trade than Sweden's, making the protective tariffs preferred by Sweden disadvantageous to Norway. Also, Norway had traditionally close trading relations with the United Kingdom, while Sweden's largest trading partners were Germany and the other countries around the Baltic Sea.

In 1895, these differences led to a prolonged crisis, the so-called "consulates question": the *Storting*'s demand that it appoint its own foreign consuls. As the king sought to maintain Sweden's dominance in foreign policy, the proposal was rejected. Yet the Norwegians continued to resist, leading to political consolidation under the anti-unionist political slogan "National Kingdom," adopted by both Høyre and Venstre.

In 1897, the disagreements over economic and trade interests caused the free trade agreement between Sweden and Norway to be revoked, which effectively erased any practical significance of the union. Even right-wing politicians in Sweden increasingly supported Norway's secession.

However, the conflict subsided somewhat after 1897, as the Scandinavianist movement briefly rose to prominence again. In 1903, Norwegian writer Bjørnstjerne Bjørnson (1832–1910) received the Nobel Prize in Literature, and Professor Sophus Bugge (1833–1907) delivered a speech on the need for new Scandinavian cooperation. In 1904, with the support of many industrialists and scientists across Scandinavia, the Nordic Economic Cooperation Association (Nordisk Förening för Ekonomiskt Samarbete) was established. Yet the Swedish–Norwegian union was not truly reinvigorated: cooperation could just as well proceed on a voluntary basis, without the unnecessary tensions caused by the union.

The status quo nevertheless remained in place until 1905, when a Norwegian coalition government of liberals and conservatives passed a definitive law on the establishment of independent Norwegian consulates. King Oscar II refused to promulgate the law, and the government resigned. However, the king did not appoint a new government, and on June 7, Norway entered a constitutional crisis. On the same day it withdrew from the union with Sweden through a declaration issued by the *Storting*.

The king's actions stirred up a storm of indignation in Sweden, with even the Social Democrats supporting Norwegian independence, and threatening to call a general strike if there was to be a military intervention. Intimidated, the king was, in principle, willing to abandon the union, but insisted on a referendum, which took place on August 13, and showed that 99.95 percent of Norwegians were in favor of secession.

Subsequent negotiations took place between Norway and Sweden on August 31, by which time European public opinion was also leaning toward the Norwegian side. Despite military readiness on both sides of the border, the talks proceeded peacefully. On October 9, the separation terms were ratified by the Norwegian *Storting*, and on October 13 by the Swedish *Riksdag*. On October 26, Oscar II abdicated the Norwegian throne. A second constitutional referendum on the future form of government took place on November 12–13 and showed that 79 percent of Norwegians wanted to retain the monarchy. As Norway now needed a new king, an offer was made to the Swedish royal house, but it was rejected by Oscar II. In the end

Haakon VII was crowned king of Norway in November 1905. He ruled until his death in 1957.

it was the Danish Prince Carl Christian Frederik Georg Valdemar Axel who, on November 27, was crowned king of Norway under the name Haakon VII (1872–1957).

In Sweden, the dissolution of the union marked the tail end of Sweden's political aspirations for the status of a regional hegemon. Going forward, there would be a greater emphasis on other forms of Swedish leadership. But more generally and importantly, Norway's regaining of independence was the first bloodless, non-coercive secession of a state to independence in modern European history: a sign for many others that their dream of breaking free from colonial rule was attainable in principle.

14

WORLD WAR I: NEUTRALITY AND POLITICAL RENEWAL

BY THE END OF THE NINETEENTH CENTURY, most of Europe had, in principle, accepted popular sovereignty: the idea that political authority derives from the consent of the governed, rather than from tradition, divine ordination or anything else. Yet the implementation of this principle remained incomplete. Even relatively small and peaceful states such as Sweden and Denmark did not adopt the parliamentary accountability principle before the early twentieth century, and universal suffrage came ten to fifteen years later still. This situation exacerbated domestic and international tensions: while liberal, and even conservative, elites felt increased pressure to act in line with public opinion—not least in matters of national interest and national honor—there was no democratic mandate to hold them accountable for their decisions and encourage moderation. In the international arena, this was a contributing factor to the arms race and the consolidation of major European states into two large alliances:

the Allies (or Entente) and the Central Powers.

In earlier times, possible or actual international conflicts could be managed through secret diplomatic channels, but the importance of public opinion made this increasingly difficult. Furthermore, contemporary geopolitical thinking had embraced the idea that Darwinist competition for survival applied to interstate relations, with stronger powers inevitably subjugating weaker ones. And, last but not least, the absence of major European wars in the second half of the nineteenth century left political, and even military, leaders uncertain about what modern warfare would entail, causing unwarranted optimism about war as an instrument of politics.

For Scandinavian states, the increasing prominence of European alliance politics strengthened their conviction to remain on the outside. Early-twentieth-century Danish foreign policy, for instance, had long been orientated toward neutrality, but there was domestic disagreement over what neutrality would mean in practice. Conservatives demanded a strong army and the construction of fortifications to deter potential aggressors, while the Social Liberals advocated for complete disarmament. Most of Danish society agreed that defense could not be ignored, especially because Denmark was right next to Germany, which in 1871 had become an empire. The more Germany militarized, the more important it was to demonstrate that a neutral Denmark would neither be hostile to Germany nor leave its territory defenseless against Germany's adversaries.

Important domestic reforms also followed. In 1915, the Danish constitution was revised in a liberal spirit: suffrage was granted to women, servants and tenant farmers, the voting age was lowered to twenty-five years, proportional representation was introduced and property qualifications were abolished.

Norway had experienced even more rapid industrial development in the years 1905–14, and by the beginning of World War I, its merchant fleet was the fourth largest in the world. Norway had also continued its tradition of liberal politics, especially as the influence of the social democrats grew. In 1907 and 1913, suffrage reforms granted women the right to vote. Other reforms of the period included labor laws protecting women and children, accident insurance for seafaring men, health insurance, a ten-hour workday and forty-eight-hour work week.

In Sweden, suffrage had become a central political issue, even before the dissolution of the union in 1905. The introduction of universal conscription in 1901 had given a further impetus to democratization, and the liberal government of Prime Minister Karl Staaff, appointed in 1905, made the extension of voter rights its priority. Universal male suffrage was put in place for the first time for the 1911 elections to the second chamber of parliament, where liberals once again emerged victorious.

Another central political issue in Sweden was national defense. The liberals had won the elections with promises to limit military spending and reduce the armed forces, so Staaff was reluctant to increase defense expenditure—even in 1913 and 1914, when the danger of war had become palpable. King Gustav V, who had ascended to the throne in 1907, took a different view, and organized a remarkable political intervention to gain public support against Staaff.

In early 1914, about 30,000 farmers, from all parts of Sweden, marched to the Royal Palace in Stockholm, where the king gave a rousing pro-defense speech. This led to a crisis of government. After lengthy negotiations, the king appointed a new right-wing cabinet under Prime Minister Hjalmar Hammarskjöld (1862–1953). The crisis could have been fatal for the Swedish monarchy if it had not been for the fact that World War I broke out just a few months later, proving that Gustav V had judged the situation more accurately than Staaff.

In early 1914, King Gustav V gave a rousing speech in support of national defense at a demonstration attended by some 30,000 farmers.

At the beginning of the war, Denmark found itself in a particularly precarious position due to its strategic location. Denmark lay at the northern tip of Germany and held control over potential British access to the Baltic Sea. It was also economically dependent on both countries for agricultural exports and the import of energy (especially coal) and raw materials. Denmark therefore decided to remain neutral and continue trading with both Germany and the United Kingdom. However, as the fate of Belgium and Luxembourg demonstrated, declarations of neutrality could not fully ensure security.

The primary threat to Denmark was the potential for a preemptive strike by Germany to secure the entrance into the Baltic Sea and prevent the United Kingdom from doing the same. Consequently, Denmark took pains not to antagonize Germany and to accommodate German demands. Nevertheless, when Germany began laying mines in Danish territorial waters without permission, a political crisis broke out, which could only be resolved by Prince Valdemar (1858–1939), the king's uncle. He convinced the government and military to accept the minefields and wrote a letter to the United Kingdom explaining Denmark's predicament. Later, Germany pressured Denmark to lay further mines themselves, but as the British Navy never attempted a breakthrough into the Baltic Sea, Denmark succeeded in maintaining its neutrality.

At the same time, the war also presented opportunities. Like other neutral countries, Denmark could go on trading with both warring parties, even if its manufacturing capacity was constrained by shortages of raw materials. Such trade, however, came with significant risks. In 1915, Germany designated all waters around Britain a war zone and announced that it was prepared to sink all ships, even neutral ships, that entered it. In 1917, German aggression escalated again, with unrestricted submarine warfare that made further trade with the United Kingdom almost impossible. Exports to Germany increased but could not compensate for lost access to the British market. Finally, it was a national tragedy for Denmark that many ethnic Danes who had become German citizens due to the annexation of Schleswig and Holstein were drafted into the German army, where nearly 4,000 of them perished.

The main Norwegian challenges were likewise related to trade. Even though Norway also declared itself neutral in 1914, its dependence on its large merchant fleet meant that the Norwegian economy came under significant pressure from both Germany and the United Kingdom. Norway's own sympathies leaned toward the United Kingdom, as its most important trading partner and source of vital coal imports. While the Venstre government under Gunnar Knudsen (1848–1928) tried to maintain the appearance of Norway's neutrality, its actual pro-British stance was quite evident.

At the same time, the United Kingdom imposed various demands on its "neutral ally," including barter agreements that could be disadvantageous and restrictions on exports to Germany, which sometimes led to German countermeasures. Due to naval blockades, imports also became challenging, leading to shortages of food and the introduction of rationing and price controls. By the war's end, German submarine warfare had caused the demise of half of Norway's merchant fleet, and the death of thousands of Norwegian sailors. But some Norwegians had also profited handsomely from wartime ventures, with risky voyages yielding high returns.

Sweden also declared itself neutral at the outset of the war and successfully retained neutrality until its end. However, Sweden's neutrality policy had a legalistic streak in the spirit of the 1907 Hague Convention, which demanded that neutrals exercise strictly equal treatment of both belligerent sides. As such neutrality mainly benefited Germany (Swedish iron ore was an important raw material in the German war effort), the Allies increasingly restricted Sweden's trade with England and the United States, before eventually ending it altogether. This affected not only Sweden's exports but also its imports, leading to food shortages and the implementation of rationing in 1916. When the United States entered the war in the spring of 1917, the situation worsened, and demonstrations broke out around the country, including mass riots in Stockholm and Gothenburg. Consequently, Hammarskjöld and his government were forced to resign, and a new right-wing government negotiated with the Allies to reopen trade.

In 1917, food shortages and rationing in Sweden led to protests around the nation, including this women's demonstration in Malmö against the price of milk.

Maintenance of neutrality was challenging for all Scandinavian countries, but they nevertheless fared remarkably well and emerged with little damage, which provided the basis for postwar economic growth. The war also created closer ties between the Scandinavian countries themselves: the neutrality declarations of all three were issued jointly, and further cooperation was coordinated at subsequent meetings of Nordic monarchs and government officials. Some joint protests were also issued, and attempts were made, albeit unsuccessfully, to mediate between the belligerents.

World War I held a special meaning for Finland, which, after more than a century as a Grand Duchy in the Russian Empire, gained independence through a series of political events and upheavals in the end stage of the war. This process had been preceded by years of growing dissatisfaction with Russian rule and agitation for national independence, but in the end it was the two 1917 Russian revolutions that opened a space for Finland to declare its independence on December 6, 1917. Nevertheless, significant tensions within Finnish society remained unresolved, and, in spring 1918, the country faced a short but brutal civil war between left-wing forces sympathetic to the Russian revolution and right-wing forces (known as "the Whites") relying on Germany.

In the end, the Whites were victorious, but during the war, a conflict arose between Finland and Sweden over the status of the Åland Islands, in the Gulf of Bothnia, which were 95 percent Swedish-speaking and had appealed to Sweden for protection. In the end, the dispute was resolved by a League of Nations commission, which left the islands to Finland but granted them a special autonomous status that has been retained to this day.

SPIES, SABOTAGE AND SMUGGLING IN NEUTRAL SCANDINAVIA

During World War I, neutral Scandinavia became a crucial hub for espionage and sabotage, as both the Allies and Central Powers attempted to exploit their strategic positions. All three Scandinavian kingdoms were infiltrated by agents from Germany, Britain and Russia, with Stockholm frequently dubbed the "spy capital of Europe." Most of these covert efforts were focused on gathering information about the enemy, but they occasionally ended up implicating local individuals, raising questions about the credibility of Scandinavian neutrality.

British intelligence established in Scandinavia a network of informants who reported on German shipping and naval maneuvers, helping the United Kingdom to successfully impose its blockade on Germany. Germany, for its part, carried out sabotage operations targeting British and Russian interests, including experiments with biological warfare (sugar cubes with embedded anthrax germs meant to be fed to transport horses) and the mining of ships with so-called coal torpedoes—bombs disguised as lumps of coal that would explode when shoveled into the furnace of a steamship. Denmark's proximity to Germany made it essential for blockade-evading smuggling of supplies across the border, including food and coal.

The Scandinavian authorities were generally aware of these activities but found it challenging to prevent them, as they attempted to uphold good relations with both belligerent sides. There were also significant logistical and manpower constraints stopping them, not least in Sweden's and Norway's remote coastal areas.

The years of World War I were also a time when some crucial foundations were laid for the development of Scandinavian welfare states. The period of unrest in the final stage of the war gave the social-democratic parties a whole new level of influence, and even many conservatives, fearing revolution, became supporters of democratization. In Sweden, nearly 600,000 people marched on May 1, 1918, demanding the abolition of the first chamber of parliament and the monarchy. On November 12, 1918, the social democratic Norwegian Labor Party called for revolutionary action and in July 1919 organized a march to support Soviet Russia. Large syndicalist demonstrations took place in Copenhagen in February and November 1918.

The revolutionary threat in Scandinavia nevertheless passed relatively quickly, as moderate social reform demands were hastily addressed. Sweden had already introduced a general state pension by 1914, and the eight-hour workday had been implemented across Scandinavia by mid-1919. Political traditions inherited from the nineteenth century, which favored peaceful public debate and reforms within existing constitutional frameworks, may have played a further role in calming revolutionary sentiment. Most importantly of all, the suffrage issue was finally solved. Important liberalizing changes to the Danish constitution had been adopted in 1915, but this didn't occur in Sweden until after the 1917 elections, when a coalition government of liberals and social democrats came to power under Prime Minister Nils Edén (1871–1945). Subsequently, universal suffrage in both parliamentary and local government elections was introduced by the 1921 elections: the first fully democratic elections in Swedish history.

15

THE INTERWAR PERIOD: CRISIS AND RECOVERY

POLITICALLY, THE SCANDINAVIAN INTERWAR period can be divided into two phases: the 1920s were characterized by short-lived, weak governments, and the 1930s by initial deep crisis, but then continuing stability. It was during this transition from crisis to stability that foundations were laid for some distinctively Scandinavian political traditions that still exercise an influence today.

The time immediately following World War I saw a rapid improvement in economic conditions in Europe as it reopened its borders for free trade, but this was soon followed by a crisis affecting the entire continent. It also revealed weaknesses in the Scandinavian economies: high inflation, trade deficits, an oversized industrial sector and a weak domestic market. Stability began to return after 1922, with the latter half of the 1920s marked by recovery. Nevertheless, workers' conditions did not significantly improve, with persistent unemployment and weakened unions due to divisions between social democrats and communists. The governments were typically minority governments or coalitions between socialists and non-socialists, with frequent elections and a tendency for political short-termism. Sharp ideological differences between socialist and non-socialist parties continued to make cooperation between them challenging.

In contrast, the 1930s saw a marked increase in stability, with socialist-dominated coalitions or socialist minority governments cooperating with centrist parties. Elections occurred at regular intervals, and there was remarkable legislative productivity. This stability can be attributed partly to the further strengthening of the social democrats, but more so to an overall greater willingness to cooperate and compromise across the socialist/non-socialist divide. At a time when anti-democratic forces were on the rise throughout Europe, Scandinavian societies succeeded in restoring national unity in a democratic way.

In Denmark, the postwar period began with a conflict between the parliament and the king over the issue of reclaiming the disputed territories from Germany. According to the Treaty of Versailles, signed in 1920, North and Central Schleswig (now Southern Jutland) were to be returned to Denmark, contingent on a popular referendum. However, while 75 percent of North Schleswig voted in favor of reunification with Denmark, Central Schleswig preferred to remain in Germany, with only 20 percent in favor of reunification. Despite this outcome, many Danish nationalists, including King Christian X (1870–1947), who had ascended to the throne in 1912, believed that Central Schleswig should also be reclaimed to weaken Germany, as it was home to Flensburg, the region's largest city.

Subsequently, Christian X ordered the Social Democrat prime minister Carl Theodor Zahle (1866–1946) to proceed with reunification with Central Schleswig. Zahle refused to comply, leading to a fierce conflict between him and the king. Subsequently, Christian X dissolved the government and put in place a conservative cabinet under Otto Liebe (1860–1929). The king's actions sparked widespread protests, threatening the future of the monarchy, until Christian X eventually reached an agreement with the Social Democrats, dismissed his replacement government and appointed a compromise cabinet to serve until the next elections. This was the last time a Danish monarch attempted to act unilaterally without parliamentary support.

Throughout the 1920s, Denmark faced economic challenges, including a crisis in the early years of the decade, followed by poor economic conditions that lasted until its second half. The bankruptcy of the country's largest bank, Landmandsbanken, and soaring unemployment in 1922 were emblematic of these difficulties. By the 1924 elections, the Social Democrats, under the leadership of Thorvald Stauning (1873–1942), had become the country's largest party, and they once again emerged victorious in the 1929 elections, forming a coalition government with the Social Liberals.

In Norway, the social democrats had demonstrated their strength in the 1915 elections but remained in the minority due to the peculiarities of the Norwegian electoral system, with the result that Venstre continued to be the leading party.

This pushed the socialists in a more radical direction, and, unlike the other Scandinavian social-democratic parties, they joined the Communist International in 1919. They left in 1923, due to disagreements with Moscow's demands.

As the economy improved in the latter half of the 1920s, Venstre was able to fulfill some of its earlier social policy promises, such as sickness and accident insurance and better availability of mortgages. In the 1918 elections, Høyre had also regained the status of a mass party, as many bourgeois voters perceived Venstre as excessively liberal or even socialist.

Norway's foreign policy in the interwar period was characterized by territorial expansion in the Arctic Circle. Through agreements with the League of Nations, in the 1920s Norway acquired the Spitsbergen islands (now known as Svalbard) and the island of Jan Mayen, while Norwegian hunters and fishermen established a foothold on parts of the eastern coast of Greenland. This led to conflict with Denmark, which continued to demand full sovereignty over Greenland, an issue that in 1933 was eventually decided in favor of Denmark by the Permanent Court of International Justice in the Hague. In 1939, Queen Maud Land, in Antarctica, was also declared Norwegian territory. This northern expansion occurred alongside the rebuilding of Norway's merchant fleet, with Norwegian shipping growing by a staggering 500 percent between 1925 and 1930.

In Sweden, the Social Democrats and the liberal Folkpartiet had collaborated in 1917–21 to realize their shared democratic ideals, but thereafter their paths diverged again, leading to the resignation of Nils Edén's coalition government in 1920.

However, the differences between liberals and conservatives remained just as significant, preventing effective coalition-building on the right of the political spectrum as well. Consequently, forming a government with majority support in parliament became almost unattainable in the 1920s, leading to a series of minority governments or unstable coalitions.

At the same time, Sweden experienced rapid industrial growth following its initial postwar crisis. New industries, relying on Swedish inventions such as Alfred Nobel's dynamite and Gustaf de Laval's (1845–1913) cream separator, expanded both domestically and internationally. Ivar Kreuger's (1880–1932) company Svenska Tändsticks enjoyed a near-global monopoly on safety matches, and companies such as Bofors, AGA, SKF, LM Ericsson and Electrolux thrived, establishing subsidiaries worldwide. Urbanization also accelerated, with two thirds of Swedes living in cities and towns by the end of World War II.

Swedish inventor Alfred Nobel, who invented dynamite in 1867.

Scandinavia's commitment to permanent neutrality remained central in the interwar period, overshadowing all other foreign policy priorities. This was not unproblematic, since all Scandinavian countries had joined the League of Nations upon its establishment in early 1920. As membership came with the obligation to enact economic, or even military, sanctions on aggressive states that breached the collective defense principle, a prolonged and inconclusive debate ensued in Scandinavia over whether such an obligation could be reconciled with neutrality.

The Great Depression, beginning with a stock market crash in the United States in 1929 and spreading worldwide, presented another significant challenge to the whole region. Remarkably, the approaches to solving it in Denmark, Norway and Sweden were all broadly alike, in each case involving successful dealmaking between social-democratic and bourgeois political forces.

The effects of the crisis reached Scandinavia in 1930. Demand for raw materials, industrial products and services dropped, leading to bankruptcies, some borrowers becoming insolvent, and others rushing to withdraw their money from banks. In the mid-1930s, unemployment reached 30 percent in Norway, 32 percent in Denmark and 24 percent in Sweden. This brought to the forefront many social tensions, which occasionally resulted in violence. In 1930, an unemployed Dane attempted to shoot the Danish minister of social affairs K.K. (Karl Kristian) Steincke (1880–1963). In 1931, the Swedish military opened fire on workers demonstrating in Ådalen, resulting in the deaths of five people.

THE BEGINNINGS OF WELFARE STATE IDEOLOGY

Before World War I, Swedish Social Democrats had struggled to gain cross-party support for their welfare agenda, as other parties naturally resisted reforms that would have primarily benefited Social Democratic voters. The electoral system at the time also prevented the Social Democrats from securing an outright parliamentary majority. Instead of further radicalization, however, these challenges led the Social Democrats to collaborate with other parties and seek to represent broader social interests than those of the working class.

By the late 1920s, a new social democratic ideology emerged, focusing on the welfare state as its core promise. The previous emphasis on class struggle and strengthening the working class at the expense of privileged groups was replaced by the new aim of developing a robust welfare system promoting equality and dignified life for all, fostering internal solidarity and national unity.

This approach required a significant degree of economic redistribution and reduced individual freedom of choice, and it involved compromising with the bourgeoisie to incorporate heightened attention to social welfare into the capitalist structures of society. Yet it proved to be a winning strategy with the voters. The concept of the state as a benevolent parental authority, and the country as a home for the people, was very appealing during the age of national unity movements across Europe.

In Sweden, this idea was encapsulated in the 1928 "The People's Home" (*Folkhemmet*) speech by Social Democratic leader Per Albin Hansson (1885–1946). In 1934, the Danish Social Democrats adopted a similar slogan, "Denmark for the People" (*Danmark for folket*). By the mid-1930s, the transition from "social relief state" to welfare state—which would provide universal, non-means-tested welfare to all—was already underway in Sweden

Swedish prime minister Per Albin Hansson giving his famous 'The People's Home' speech in 1928.

and Denmark. Norway followed suit, with the social democrats coming to power in 1935.

Concerns over declining fertility rates were an important reason these ideas gained broad acceptance. As in developed Western European countries, birth rates had been dropping in Scandinavia since the early twentieth century, and active social policies were seen as a way of encouraging childbirth and raising good citizens. Concrete ways to accomplish this were proposed by social scientists, such as the Swedish couple Gunnar and Alva Myrdal (1898–1987; 1902–86) in their 1934 book *Kris i befolkningsfrågan* (Crisis in the Population Question). In 1935, Denmark and Sweden initiated national population surveys to explore ways to ensure better living conditions. The recommendations included establishing kindergartens, providing low-interest housing loans, improving sexual education and providing welfare support for expectant mothers. Some of these measures began to be implemented in the latter half of the 1930s.

This new belief in state-led social management somewhat revived the progressive optimism lost in the turmoil of World War I. It also elevated the public role of experts, including female social scientists such as Alva Myrdal, in Sweden, and Aase Lionæs (1907–99), in Norway. In the 1930s, scientific institutes were established to study previously private matters such as household chores, marriage and childcare. Concepts such as living spaces, health, nutrition and hygiene became measurable and regulated, with the state assuming responsibility for their improvement.

When the United Kingdom abandoned the pound sterling's gold standard in 1931, Denmark followed suit, undermining confidence in the national currency. In 1932, special tariffs were imposed on colonial trade, forcing certain goods to be bought and sold at fixed prices. These measures were intended to alleviate the crisis but ultimately ended up exacerbating its effects. Nevertheless, the Social Democratic government was able to act decisively in agreement with their Social Liberal coalition partners. Foreign trade was put under strict control, the Danish krone was devalued, and wage agreements were frozen. In turn, the Social Liberals lent their support to the Social Democrats' program of social reforms, which included old-age pensions and health, unemployment and occupational accident insurance.

This compromise agreement (known as Kanslergadeforliget), in which each partner made concessions to the other's program to alleviate the crisis and keep the government in place, was hugely successful. As unpopular decisions were balanced with popular ones, the Social Democrats succeeded in winning the 1935 elections again, and the coalition of socialists and radicals gained a majority in both chambers of the parliament. At the same time, foreign trade picked up again, and, by the late 1930s, industry was expanding once more.

The agreement served as a model for the rest of Scandinavia as well. In the same year, the Swedish Social Democrats, led by Per Albin Hansson, and their centrist coalition partners, the Farmers' League (Bondeförbundet), reached a similar agreement.

Sweden had been hit by the Great Depression as severely as

other European countries. An early peak of the crisis was the shooting at the labor demonstrations in Ådalen in May 1931, mentioned above, a tragedy that became a symbol of the labor movement's demands for freedom and the right to strike. Former Social Democratic prime minister Rickard Sandler (1884–1964) delivered a speech at the victims' funeral.

A scene from the Ådalen labour demonstration of May 14, 1931. Several minutes later, the Swedish military opened fire, killing five people.

In the spring of 1932, tensions escalated further when industrialist Ivar Kreuger committed suicide in Paris. Kreuger, who had controlled much of the world's safety match market, was found to have borrowed hundreds of millions of Swedish crowns and lent them to other companies, believing that he was contributing to global economic growth. Additionally, Kreuger had forged promissory notes worth £21 million. Panic ensued, and the Swedish stock market closed for a week to prevent a crash. Partially due to this scandal, the Social Democrats won a landslide victory in the 1932 parliamentary elections and formed a minority government under Per Albin Hansson, promising to actively combat unemployment, in the style of the American New Deal, through the organization of large-scale public relief works, where workers would receive competitive wages rather than unemployment benefits.

To implement this strategy against the opposition of right-wing parties, whose program—to save public money, rather than spend it—was diametrically opposed to theirs, the Social Democrats sought support from the Farmers' League. A successful agreement was reached whereby the latter supported the Social Democrats' employment policies, while the Social Democrats agreed to introduce agricultural subsidies. The same cooperation continued even after the subsequent elections in 1936, resulting in the first Swedish government since the 1920s to have majority support in the parliament. Meanwhile, the economy had started to grow again, and unemployment was decreasing.

Until 1935, all governing parties in Norway (the conservatives, liberals and agrarians) supported a liberal economic policy. By 1927, unemployment had risen to a fifth of the working-age population, and it increased even more with the onset of the Great Depression. Yet the governments led by agrarians (1931–33) and Venstre (1933–35) sought to combat the crisis solely by reducing government spending and refusing expansionist fiscal policies and emergency relief measures proposed by the social democrats. By 1933, at the peak of the crisis, at least a third of Norway's workforce was unemployed.

In 1935, the social democrats, led by Johan Nygaardsvold (1879–1952), formed a minority government with the support of the agrarian Bondepartiet. Just as had happened in Sweden, the agrarian party supported the social democrats' social program, which included pension reforms, industrial reforms, new public holidays and unemployment insurance, financed through higher taxes and increased public investment. Although unemployment was slow to go down, by 1938 the situation had markedly improved.

Thanks to political agreements and willingness to compromise, political tensions in Scandinavia decreased during the recovery from the Great Depression. Strikes practically ended in the second half of the 1930s, and the authority of the state, which had declined during the era of 1920s minority governments, improved again. Going forward, the state took on an active role in facilitating deal-making between employers' and workers' organizations. In 1935, the employers and trade unions in Norway signed the Hovedavtalen, or Basic Agreement, and, in 1938, Sweden followed with the Saltsjöbadsavtalet, regulating the mutual relationships and conflict resolution mechanisms.

Arguably, the economic situation in Scandinavia would have improved by the second half of the 1930s in any case, exposed as the small Scandinavian economies were to Europe-wide fluctuations. Therefore, the measures taken to solve the crisis also had a psychological, and not purely economic, significance: people felt that the new policy of increased state intervention had produced much-needed relief and were therefore more prepared to accept state intervention in other areas of life. In the end, this contributed to a general understanding of the duty of the state as not just to enforce the law and defend liberal rights but also to ensure the well-being of its citizens. Compared to most of the rest of Europe, where the Great Depression caused a widespread turn toward authoritarianism, the 1930s developments in Scandinavia were highly atypical, quickly becoming a source of national pride.

16

WORLD WAR II: RESISTANCE AND ACQUIESCENCE

IN THE INTERWAR PERIOD, Nordic foreign policy had a purely defensive orientation. The social democrats, who by the mid-1930s were the dominant political force, had initially favored disarmament, but in the tense atmosphere of the 1930s, even they became more amenable to investing in national defense.

Scandinavian defense policy had been dependent on the League of Nations as a guarantor of their neutrality. However, as the League of Nations proved unable to restrain Italy's aggression in Abyssinia and Hitler's open violation of the Versailles Treaty in 1936, Scandinavia's faith in the organization was undermined. Wary of being dragged into another war between the European great powers, the Scandinavian states announced that they no longer considered themselves bound by the League of Nations' sanctions regime.

To compensate, Sweden initiated negotiations in 1938 regarding the possible establishment of a Nordic defense alliance. Denmark and Norway, however, were not amenable to these plans. Norway preferred to maintain strict neutrality and, along with Sweden, rejected Nazi Germany's offer of a non-aggression pact in 1939. Denmark, still careful to avoid arousing suspicions that it was aligning itself with Germany's enemies, decided to accept a similar offer in the same year.

Finland had sought regional allies in the early interwar period as an insurance policy against possible Soviet aggression, but it later adopted a policy of neutrality as well. This, however, did little to alleviate the Soviet threat. After the signing of the Soviet–German Molotov–Ribbentrop Pact in August 1939, the secret protocol of which allocated Finland to the Soviet sphere of influence, the Soviet Union presented an ultimatum to Finland. Unlike the Baltic states, which accepted Soviet demands, Finland refused to do so and was invaded by the Red Army three months later.

In the ensuing Winter War, the outnumbered Finnish forces, led by Marshal Carl Gustaf Emil Mannerheim (1867–1951), employed innovative guerrilla tactics and used the harsh winter conditions to their advantage, inflicting significant casualties on the Soviet side. After several months of hostilities, the Moscow Peace Treaty was eventually signed on March 12, 1940. Although Finland retained its independence, it suffered significant territorial losses, including all its possessions in the Karelian Isthmus. As an aggressor, the Soviet Union was expelled from the League of Nations but otherwise faced few international consequences. Finland's immediate neighbors Sweden and Norway maintained their strict neutrality during the war, refusing the transit of British and French troops and equipment over their territory. Nevertheless, numerous Swedes volunteered to help Finland, and there was an outpouring of sympathy for the Finnish cause.

This pro-Finnish propaganda poster urged Swedes to join Finland's forces during the Winter War.

Finland subsequently attempted to regain lost territory as an ally of Nazi Germany in the Continuation War of June 1941 to September 1944. Despite its efforts, the borders established in the 1940 peace treaty were reaffirmed in 1944.

The next foreign state to invade the Nordics was Nazi Germany, which claimed to believe that Danish and Norwegian neutrality was not credible, and the region therefore constituted a security vulnerability. Indeed, in February 1940, the British Navy intercepted a German ship in Norwegian waters and freed the British prisoners of war it had been carrying. This incident highlighted Norway's inability to defend its neutrality.

In April 1940, the United Kingdom went further and decided to mine Norwegian waters to disrupt Swedish iron ore shipments to Germany. However, Germany invaded both Denmark and Norway just a few days later. At the postwar Nuremberg trials, this invasion was deemed illegal, as German leaders had not perceived any imminent threat of Allied occupation of Norway.

The invasion began on the morning of April 9, 1940. Denmark capitulated swiftly and accepted German "protection," with a new national unity government formed by Thorvald Stauning. In Norway, Germany faced more resistance. Although the phase of active combat there was relatively brief, with the last Norwegian forces surrendering on June 10, the invasion was decapitated in the beginning of the attack, as the German cruiser *Blücher*, carrying the entire German operational leadership, was sunk north of Norway's Oscarsborg Fortress. This allowed the Norwegian king, government and members of the *Storting* time to evacuate.

Norway's King Haakon VII and the Nygaardsvold government established themselves in London exile, where they coordinated national resistance. Norway's merchant fleet was handed over to the Allies, and an exile Norwegian army was formed, eventually comprising nearly 14,000 men. Fearful of a counterattack, Germany was forced to maintain a substantial force of approximately 400,000 troops in Norway, depriving the other fronts of reinforcements. At the same time, Germany's occupation of Norway made the invasion of Sweden an easier prospect, which put Sweden under significant pressure to make various concessions to German interests.

THE HEAVY-WATER SABOTAGE

The Norwegian heavy-water sabotage (Tungtvannsaksjonen) was a series of British–Norwegian covert operations carried out during World War II with the aim of disrupting Nazi Germany's development of nuclear weapons. This was accomplished by targeting heavy-water production facilities in occupied Norway, with a primary focus on the Vemork hydroelectric plant near Rjukan, in the Telemark region. This was the first site in the world to mass-produce heavy water (deuterium), a critical component for nuclear reactors.

In Operation Grouse (October 1942), a British Special Operations Executive (SOE) team successfully inserted four Norwegian commandos onto the Hardangervidda plateau to prepare for subsequent missions. Operation Freshman, which followed in November, involved British paratroopers who were to rendezvous with the Grouse team and proceed to Vemork. However, this attempt failed when their gliders crashed short of their destination, resulting in the deaths, or capture and subsequent execution, of the saboteurs. Finally, in Operation Gunnerside (February 1943), a team of SOE-trained Norwegian commandos successfully infiltrated the Vemork plant and destroyed its heavy-water production facility.

Following these instances of sabotage, the Germans attempted to transport the remaining heavy water to Germany, but in February 1944 Norwegian resistance forces successfully sank the SF *Hydro*, the ferry carrying the heavy water, on Lake Tinn. These efforts ultimately prevented Nazi Germany from developing nuclear weapons during the war and are still celebrated today.

The Norwegian coast was also well suited as a base for submarine warfare in the North Atlantic.

Denmark was exploited by the German authorities in a different way: it was treated comparatively well from the beginning and, in fact, turned into a form of model occupation, which held significant propaganda value. Formally, Denmark remained an independent state, but anti-German newspapers were banned, and Danish communists were sent to concentration camps in 1941. The following year, a secret resistance movement rose to prominence, leading German forces to seize power throughout the country and form their own government. However, King Christian X remained the head of state, and Danish political institutions continued to operate, although real decision-making power lay with the German authorities.

Danish Nazis hardly played any role in local governance, but in Norway, where the country's leadership had escaped, the situation was different. The Germans initially sought cooperation with traditional political elites, but when these efforts failed, they made the far-right Norwegian Nasjonal Samling, under its leader, Vidkun Quisling (1887–1945), the sole permitted political party. Still, Norway's Nazification faced an uphill struggle and was strongly resisted by civil society organizations, such as sports clubs, trade unions and the church. In 1942, for instance, all Norwegian bishops resigned in protest from their offices as church administrators. An armed resistance movement also emerged and had some remarkable successes, such as the sabotage of the Vemork hydroelectric plant in 1943.

At the same time, Norwegians and Danes were internally divided between their right- and left-wing factions, which influenced their attitude toward the occupation. Among right-wing politicians, there was some fear of the resistance movement, as it was seen as a breeding ground for communism. In Sweden, police forces from Denmark and Norway were secretly being trained to be used both against Germany and to prevent the seizure of power by communists at the end of the war. Many Danish and Norwegian politicians were far from sure of a complete Nazi German defeat, and they expected to maintain a relationship with Germany after the war.

Some Norwegians and Danes had also been directly supportive of the Nazis before the war, especially in the latter half of the 1930s. At its peak, Nasjonal Samling had 40,000 members, and over 5,000 Norwegians and 4,000 Danes fought voluntarily on the German side. Several incidents associated with collaboration, such as writer Knut Hamsun's (1859–1952) expressions of support for the Nazis, remain sensitive topics to this day.

Approximately 3,600 people were killed in Denmark and 10,000 in Norway during the German occupation. About 900 Norwegian Jews, around half of Norway's Jewish population, managed to escape to Sweden, while around 700 perished. In Denmark, the plans to initiate anti-Jewish actions in February 1943 were leaked, allowing for the escape of around 7,000 Danish Jews to Sweden, while fifty-two Danish Jews are known to have died in concentration camps.

Sweden was the only Nordic country to successfully retain its neutrality during World War II. Yet its experiences in the two world wars had significant differences. In World War II, economic warfare played a somewhat diminished role, largely due to Germany's increased resilience: it had prepared for the war by stockpiling essential resources, and it benefited from trade with the Soviet Union until June 1941. Germany furthermore bolstered its economy through early conquests in Europe, resulting in a larger domestic economic base. This German hegemony over much of Europe—and crucially, in Sweden's case, over Denmark, Norway and, later, Finland—also meant that neutral countries complied less with Allied demands in the face of overwhelming German strength.

Sweden's wartime neutrality policy aimed to keep the country out of the conflict at all costs, which was understandable, given that its readiness for war, especially in 1940, was no better than Denmark's or Norway's. The situation in Sweden therefore remained tense, with constant fear of German invasion and a significant portion of the male population mobilized into the army.

At the outset of the war, Per Albin Hansson's Social Democratic government was reorganized into a broad coalition government, including all parliamentary parties except for the communists. This government made considerable efforts to avoid antagonizing the belligerents and, especially, Germany. Anti-Nazi journalists and politicians were closely monitored, communist leaders were called up for military service or interned, and various German wishes—the transport of their troops across Swedish territory, for instance—were granted. Sweden also did not strongly protest the occupation of Denmark and Norway, which upset the Norwegians in particular.

At the same time, Sweden had a great strategic interest in Finland, which it sought to maintain as a buffer between itself and the Soviet Union. Especially during the Winter War, a broad pro-Finnish movement in Sweden had organized multifaceted support for its neighbor. Sweden's engagement decreased during the Continuation War, but Sweden played an active role in negotiating the peace terms between Finland and the Soviet Union in 1944. In the aftermath of the war, Sweden accepted 50,000 Finnish refugees, as well as many Latvians and Estonians. Today, a number of Swedes with Baltic roots, such as the geneticist and Nobel laureate Svante Pääbo (1955–), have found international renown.

In 1943, some 7,000 Danish Jews fled German-occupied Denmark for Sweden. Pictured here are four siblings on the day of their arrival in Sweden, on October 6.

Another part of the Nordic region affected by occupations were Denmark's North Atlantic possessions. Germany's occupation of Denmark immediately put Iceland, the Faroe Islands and Greenland in a precarious position, even if they themselves remained untouched by German forces.

THE RESCUE OF DANISH JEWS AND THE ACTIVITIES OF RAOUL WALLENBERG

During World War II, Sweden played a crucial role in the effort to rescue the Jewish population of Denmark from the Holocaust. The German plan to deport Denmark's Jewish population was set for October 1, 1943. However, Danish resistance groups and some German informants leaked details of the plan, allowing for an escape operation to be prepared.

Over the following weeks, roughly 7200 Danish Jews, along with about 700 of their non-Jewish family members and close associates, crossed the Øresund Strait into Sweden, thanks to local fishermen and other boat owners who risked their lives to transport the escapees to safety, with police and local officials often turning a blind eye or offering discreet assistance. Of those who attempted to flee, around 500 were captured and deported. However, thanks to subsequent diplomatic efforts, most of them survived the war.

Neutral Sweden's decision to grant asylum to the Danish Jews amounted to a decisive moral stance. The same stance was evident in the actions of Swedish diplomat Raoul Wallenberg (1912–47), stationed in Hungary, who in late 1944 issued protective passports to thousands of Jews, saving them from deportation. In January 1945, during the Siege of Budapest by the Red Army, Wallenberg was detained on charges of espionage, and subsequently disappeared into the Soviet system of prison camps. He was likely executed in 1947.

The local Faroese authority, the Løgting, had declared on April 10, 1940 that, unlike Denmark, it had no intention of capitulating to Germany. This, however, did not mean it could stay out of the war. On April 12, the United Kingdom occupied the defenceless islands, and while the Løgting formally protested the occupation, in reality it cooperated with it. The British military became a major employer on the islands, and the Faroese gained access to the large English fish market. Furthermore, the Løgting assumed legislative authority, as Denmark was under occupation. However, despite calls from independence activists to seize the opportunity and declare Faroese independence, the majority voted to maintain ties with Denmark in the 1943 elections. At the same time as this was all happening, many Faroese fishing boats were sunk by the Germans, and the islands suffered human losses that were proportionate to those of the United Kingdom.

At the onset of the German occupation of Denmark, Greenland's two Danish governors initially took power into their own hands, as they were meant to do, according to Danish legislation. However, Greenland's actual fate was determined by the Danish ambassador in Washington, Henrik Kauffmann (1888–1963), who independently signed a treaty with the United States in 1941, granting the Americans permission to establish military bases in Greenland. As Greenland carried a significant strategic importance in defending the North American continent, a US military presence was soon established. For Greenlanders, the presence of a small American contingent did not have much significance. However, the war provided Greenland with some experience in self-governance, and it fostered trade with the United States and Canada.

Iceland had enjoyed independence in everything but foreign policy since 1918, and after the onset of Denmark's occupation it formed a broad coalition government, with the conservative politician Sveinn Björnsson (1881–1952) elected the regent, as Christian X was unable to perform his constitutional duties. The United Kingdom immediately offered to defend Iceland, but Iceland declined, citing its neutrality. In response, the United Kingdom initiated occupation anyway, beginning on May 10, 1940.

Subsequently, the British troops were replaced by the Canadians and then the Americans. In 1941, the United States turned Iceland into an air base for the refueling of planes on their journey to Europe. Significant construction was undertaken to establish the necessary infrastructure, unemployment nearly disappeared in Iceland, and the fishing export industry thrived. The war years were thus successful for Iceland, but the occupation was unpopular and led to domestic political tensions, especially the radicalization of the labor movement. In response, the right-wing parties organized around a program of full Icelandic independence, culminating in a referendum in 1944, in which 95 percent of the votes cast were in favor of establishing a republic.

The liberation of Norway and Denmark in late 1944 and early 1945 was mostly bloodless. Soviet forces attacked Finnmark, in northern Norway, in autumn of 1944, clearing the area of German troops. German forces in Denmark surrendered on May 5, and in Norway on May 8, 1945, handing over authority to civilian governments. The island of Bornholm was an exception, as its German commander refused to surrender, which led to a Soviet attack on the island. The Soviet troops left Finnmark in September 1945 and Bornholm in April 1946.

In the end, the Nordic countries emerged from World War II relatively intact compared to most of the rest of Europe. Even Finland, which had suffered the most, nevertheless escaped the fate of neighboring Baltic states. Whether this outcome was the result of their own merits or of a coincidence of circumstances can be debated, but it was nonetheless a victory for democracy in a world where it was scarce.

17

THE COLD WAR AND THE NORDIC BALANCE

THE DIFFERENT EXPERIENCES OF THE Nordics in World War II came to be reflected in their security policy choices during the Cold War. Sweden continued the neutrality course that had already served it well. Finland also called itself neutral, but did so more reluctantly, its options limited by the Soviet overlay. Denmark and Norway, which had been occupied by Nazi Germany, became founding members of NATO but remained somewhat less than fully committed to their membership. Iceland, a country with no standing army, also became a founding NATO member. The security configuration that thus came into being is known as the Nordic Balance. During the Cold War, it was an undoubted success story, as it helped to avoid escalation of tensions in a part of Europe that had been split by the Iron Curtain.

For the couple of years immediately following World War II, Denmark, Norway and Sweden followed a policy of "neutralism within the United Nations"—a form of continuation of their 1930s neutrality policies. At the same time, the heightening of East–West tensions suggested that isolationism was not tenable in the long term. During the Berlin blockade of June 1948 to May 1949, the Swedish foreign secretary Östen Undén (1886–1974) was tipped off by his Norwegian counterpart that Norway would revise its previous foreign policy and "open up to the West." In response, Sweden tried to propose an alternative and initiated talks with Denmark and Norway about establishing a Scandinavian defense alliance. The idea was that the Scandinavian states could isolate themselves from superpower competition by issuing a common declaration of neutrality, which would be reinforced with military strength.

Norway, which had received substantial help from the Allies during the war, was opposed to this idea, fearing that the American response would be unfavorable and lead to alienation between Norway and the Western allies. Therefore, Norway wanted the proposed alliance to establish official collaboration with the Western powers, but this was of course incompatible with Sweden's preference for neutrality. Denmark, which had experienced a much milder form of German occupation, was more open to the defense alliance idea, even without Norway, but Sweden had become skeptical, believing a Swedish–Danish alliance would be too weak and still come under the influence of NATO. The plans were therefore shelved.

This led to Denmark and Norway joining NATO when it was established in 1949. Both nevertheless tried to limit their engagement to reduce the provocative impact on the Soviet Union. A few weeks before joining, Norway decided it would not allow foreign bases on its territory in peacetime, and

Denmark adopted a similar restriction in 1953. This policy was extended in 1957, when Denmark and Norway declared they would reject the placement of nuclear weapons on their territory. Furthermore, Norway adopted a policy of "voluntary demilitarization" of the area close to the Soviet border to avoid sending any threatening signals to the Soviets. Both countries also had a strong pacifist and neutralist opposition, which in Denmark's case was reflected in the fact that it had one of the lowest defense budgets in the whole of NATO.

A demonstration against the proposed stationing of nuclear weapons in Norway in the 1950s.

Iceland's NATO membership grew directly out of its Allied occupation during World War II. The Americans were reluctant to leave after the war, and the Icelandic government agreed in 1946 that the Keflavík air base would continue to be used by the US Air Force. The base, which had been used for intermediate landings and refueling between America and Europe, was also ideally located for naval reconnaissance against Soviet submarines. In 1951, Iceland went a step further and entered into a bilateral defense agreement with the United States, with America formally taking responsibility for Iceland's defense. As Iceland thus became dependent on the United States, it never established its own defense force apart from some patrol boats.

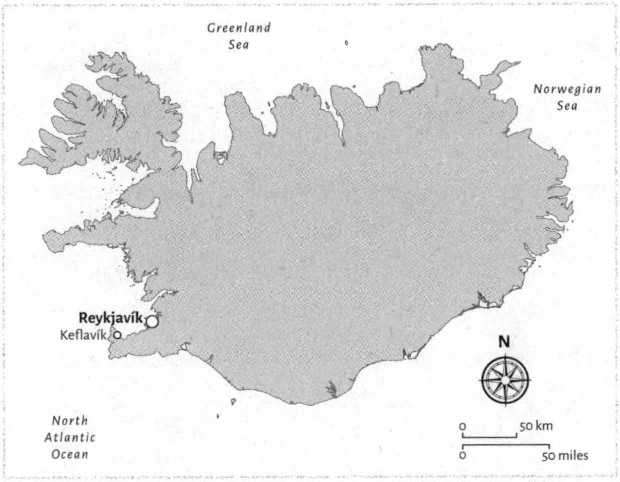

US military forces used Iceland's Keflavík until 2006.

The collapse of the Scandinavian defense alliance proposal left Sweden to pursue its traditional neutrality course alone, supported by a relatively strong military. But Sweden also undertook secret preparations for joint action with NATO in the event of an attack from the Soviet Union, a cooperation that was already established in the early 1950s.

THE COD WARS

Between 1958 and 1976, Iceland engaged in three maritime conflicts with the United Kingdom, known as the Cod Wars. The conflicts were over the extent of Iceland's exclusive fishing rights in the North Atlantic, with Iceland progressively extending its exclusive economic zone (EEZ) from 4 nautical miles to 12, then 50 and, ultimately, 200 nautical miles, each time imposing the new limits on foreign fishing vessels. This in turn provoked opposition from the United Kingdom.

The First Cod War (1958–61) began with Iceland's first unilateral EEZ extension, leading to the United Kingdom deploying warships to protect its trawlers. The incidents included Iceland's *Ægir* patrol boat ramming HMS *Russell* and warning shots being fired. An agreement was eventually reached, recognizing Iceland's 12-mile zone.

The Second Cod War (1972–73) saw Iceland expand its EEZ to 50 miles, again resulting in clashes with British and West German fleets. Icelandic patrol boats cut the nets of British trawlers, leading the United Kingdom to increase its military presence. The conflict eventually de-escalated with NATO's intervention, allowing limited British access within the 50-mile boundary.

During the Third Cod War (1975–76), Iceland extended its EEZ to 200 miles, which again caused intense confrontations with British ships. Iceland prevailed by threatening to close the NATO base at Keflavík, and the United Kingdom conceded, marking Iceland's ultimate success in this unusual attempt at Cold War–era expansionism.

It seems that NATO was willing to defend Sweden with nuclear weapons, if necessary, since Sweden was strategically important to the defense of Norway and the northern Atlantic. This arguably two-faced attitude on Sweden's part has been associated with the idea of "small-state realism," meaning that small states cannot, in the end, really afford to be idealistic about their security policy, as they rely on stronger powers to protect them.

In the immediate post–World War II decades, Sweden had by far the strongest military of all the Scandinavian states. By the mid-1970s, however, as the growth of the Swedish economy was slowing down, its defense expenditure began to decline. This did not go unnoticed by the Soviet Union, and a series of Soviet submarine incidents ensued in Swedish territorial waters in the early to mid-1980s. The most dramatic of them involved a submarine that ran aground near the Karlskrona naval base, in southeast Sweden, clearly showing Sweden's vulnerability to Soviet aggression. Still, there was no fundamental revision of Sweden's neutrality policy.

The Nordic country most exposed to Soviet influence was Finland. Following its defeat in the Continuation War, Finland signed a friendship and mutual assistance treaty with the Soviet Union in 1948, which compelled it to remain outside of "antagonistic great power interests"—that is, to refrain from entering any Western defense pacts. At the time, the USSR was keen to promote "neutrality" in its neighborhood as a way of preventing NATO encroachment. This policy reached its peak in 1952, with a proposal to reunite and neutralize Germany, distancing it from the Western Bloc. However, while promoting neutrality as a strategy, the USSR did not extend the same option to Eastern Bloc states. This was evidenced by its crushing of the 1956 uprising in Hungary, which had denounced the Warsaw Pact and declared the country neutral.

The Finnish–Soviet treaty did not include a military agreement of the type found in Soviet friendship pacts with Hungary and Romania, and, therefore, Finland did not become a part of the Eastern Bloc. Yet Finnish diplomats still struggled to build international credibility for its "neutrality." This was made particularly awkward by the fact that even though the 1948 treaty stated that neither state would interfere in the domestic affairs of the other, the Soviets did, in fact, interfere in Finnish domestic politics, not least to prop up Finland's long-serving president Urho Kaleva Kekkonen (1900–86), who was known for his "preventive diplomacy"—that is, consulting Moscow in advance of any important decisions to avoid an adverse reaction. In Finnish history, this era is known as "Finlandization."

To summarize, the Nordic Balance security configuration that emerged in the Baltic Sea region in the early 1950s was composed of Denmark and Norway as somewhat low-key members of NATO, Sweden as a non-aligned state and Finland as a not-quite-neutral state, who was in some ways beholden to the Soviet Union. These different set-ups recognized the powerful influence of both superpowers, as well as the varying security needs of the Nordic states involved. The balance could almost be regarded as a form of unspoken regional cooperation, which proved largely sustainable throughout the Cold War.

Soviet head of state Kliment Voroshilov, Communist Party first secretary Nikita Khrushchev and Finnish president Urho Kaleva Kekkonen in 1960. Kekkonen was known for consulting Moscow in advance of making important decisions.

The main aim of all the Nordics was to maintain peace. It was assumed that if the balance in the region was changed by one superpower, there would follow corresponding steps by the other, leading to escalation. Of course, the overwhelmingly more powerful of the two in the Baltic Sea region was the Soviet Union, which meant that the Nordics walked a fine line between deterring Soviet aggression and reassuring the Soviets that they would not align too closely with the West.

The permanence of these "balanced" relations was also the basis of a compelling narrative of peacefulness for the international public. As the Scandinavian countries were careful to not upset the regional power balance, they became known for their foreign policy activism in other parts of the world, where they advocated for democratic principles, rule of law and peaceful conflict resolution. From the 1960s onward, Sweden, in particular, adopted a policy of "activist internationalism," characterized by support for peace initiatives, democratization and economic development in the developing world, backed by a generous foreign-aid budget. Positioning itself as a mediator and bridge-builder between East and West, North and South, Sweden sought to attain a prestigious status on the global stage and to safeguard its own security and territorial integrity by promoting global stability through activism, just as it attempted to promote regional stability through passivism.

THE NORDIC NEUTRALS' ACTIVIST INTERNATIONALISM

Finland and Sweden, small neutral states in a potentially precarious security position, sought positive roles as mediators in the polarized world of the Cold War. Some of these attempts were remarkably fruitful. Notably, they played a significant part in the success of the Conference on Security and Co-operation in Europe (CSCE), which convened in Helsinki in 1973–75. Originally proposed by Soviet foreign minister Vyacheslav Molotov in 1954, the initiative aimed to foster European security discussions without American involvement, thus splitting the Western allies. As such, the idea initially led nowhere, but Finland made use of its credibility as a neutral state to resurrect the proposal in 1969. With thirty-five participating countries, including a loose grouping of neutral and non-aligned states known as N+N, the CSCE successfully served as a platform for mediation between the Eastern and Western Blocs.

The Helsinki Final Act of 1975, the agreement that was the end product of the CSCE, acknowledged Europe's post–World War II borders, but also demanded from all parties respect for universal freedoms and human rights, a crucial Soviet concession that was subsequently weaponized against the regime by domestic dissidents. The N+N proved instrumental in making the CSCE a success, offering Sweden and Finland a significant voice in continental affairs and underscoring the important role they could play as neutrals. However, the CSCE failed to evolve into a "mini-UN," as some neutral politicians had envisioned, highlighting the limited extent to which neutral states could shape European security discussions.

18

THE CLASSIC ERA OF THE WELFARE STATE

AFTER WORLD WAR II, NORDICS were characterized by foreign policy differences, but they also shared significant domestic political similarities. The welfare state model, which had been introduced in the late 1930s, came to its full influence after the war. The decades that followed were notable for their high degree of political consensus around what was increasingly known as "the Nordic model." This consensus ensured the long-term electoral dominance of the social democrats, and led to the development of the most advanced social welfare systems in the world.

Scandinavia was able to massively benefit from the post-war economic boom. This was particularly the case for neutral Sweden, which still had its industries intact, but Denmark and Norway were soon reconstructed. A long uninterrupted period of growth followed, lasting from the early 1950s until 1973. It saw the development of an extensive and costly state-managed network of social support systems that was largely maintained in the 1970s and 1980s. The welfare provisions made available to all included health care, health and accident insurance, child, family and housing benefits and much more. Collective agreements between employers and trade unions also put in place unemployment benefits, national holidays, workplace supervision and high pensions. Political stability and economic growth supported cultural development, improved educational opportunities, national infrastructure development and the overall well-being of the population.

A modern high-rise residential area in Tensta, Stockholm, in 1971. Tensta was built between 1966 and 1972 to provide housing for the growing population of the capital.

Notably, the convergence of a booming economy and the wide availability of childcare and aged care enabled many more women to seek paid employment in the labor market, which further encouraged the loosening of traditional gender roles, making the Scandinavian countries longstanding front-runners in terms of gender equality. This also created a positive feedback loop for the welfare state, as many of these women were employed in the expanding care sector.

Education reforms in the 1950s and 1960s fully democratized the school system, making nine or ten years of education compulsory for everyone, regardless of gender, origin or economic means. A number of new universities were established across Scandinavia (in Ålborg, Odense, Roskilde, Bergen, Trondheim, Tromsø, Umeå and Linköping), many of which experimented with innovative research and non-traditional curricula. Emphasis was also placed on continuing education, adult retraining and adult education in general.

As a result of all this, in the latter half of the twentieth century the average quality of life in the Nordic countries rose higher than almost anywhere else in the world. In the eyes of admiring foreign observers, Scandinavia became a prime example of the possibility of a "third way" between capitalism and communism, with the state functioning as a mediator between economic growth and the well-being of the population, ensuring that the former benefited the latter, but that the latter wouldn't undermine the former.

But alongside all the positive measures were some harmful ones: the Nordic model of the welfare state also intersected with ideas about eugenics and sterilization, which some saw as a valid way to improve the population and thus enhance the overall health of society. From as early as the 1930s, experts had been advocating the compulsory sterilization of individuals who were seen as less valuable and as a "burden on society" for reasons that could easily veer into forms of racism, ableism and sexism. In Sweden, in particular, involuntary sterilization of "inferior" individuals was more widespread and went on for longer than anywhere else in the West, ceasing only in 1976. By that point, more than 30,000 people had been sterilized against their will based on their perceived low value as members of society.

The success of the welfare state was possible due to the electoral dominance of the social democrats. In Denmark they were in power from 1929 to 1945, 1947 to 1973 and then 1975 to 1982. In Sweden, they were in government for an unprecedented forty-four years, from 1932 to 1976 and then again from 1982 to 1991. In Norway, they held power for thirty years, from 1935 to 1965, and then from 1973 to 1981. However, the consensus behind the welfare state was broad and involved other political forces. Usually, the social democrats did not have an outright majority, but governed either as a minority government, or in coalition with the communist or centrist/agrarian parties. To a large degree, the success of the welfare state program can be explained by the social democrats' ability to make their ideology work with those of the other political forces, and thus to become identified with the national interest.

The state continued to take a particularly active role in mediating collective labor agreements between employers' organizations and trade unions, which improved its ability to steer the economy through economic cycles. For their part, the employers accepted responsibility for providing decent benefits and retraining opportunities for the unemployed, and in exchange they received concessions from the unions on salaries, thereby avoiding a situation where rising wages would lead to rising prices and, eventually, to an economic downturn as companies would become uncompetitive on the international market. The willingness of both sides of the labor market to smooth out the economic cycles for mutual benefit became something of a trademark of Scandinavian corporatism.

In the 1950s and 1960s, the political consensus behind the welfare system was such that the influential Swedish journalist and historian Herbert Tingsten (1896–1973) even spoke in 1955 about "the end of ideology." But of course, what sustained it was not ideological consensus alone, but ongoing redistribution of wealth. The average Nordic citizen paid over 50 percent of their income in taxes, and in Sweden, self-employed individuals had to pay taxes for earnings above a certain threshold that could in some circumstances exceed 100 percent. Value-added tax was over 20 percent, and excise taxes on alcohol, tobacco and fuel were high as well; they were primarily moralistic taxes, meant to limit consumption, which was criticized as an infringement on personal freedoms.

Arguably, the welfare state system more generally stifled individual initiative, entrepreneurship and even freedom of choice. Right-wing critics argued that welfare programs relying on society's willingness to put up with high taxes inevitably faced declining credibility. While social support was guaranteed at the national level, and for everyone, the connection between rights and obligations faded, as the latter had become abstract. Many came to perceive state assistance as a first rather than a last resort, and all manner of schemes were devised to exploit the system for personal gain.

NORDIC CINEMA

In the classic era of the welfare state, Nordic cinema found international success for its artistic films characterized by psychological depth, existential themes and stark depictions of Scandinavian natural landscapes. This critical and commercial success of the films built upon the foundations laid by earlier figures such as the actress Greta Garbo (1905–90) and director Victor Sjöström (1879–1960). Born in Sweden, Garbo became an international icon in 1920s and '30s Hollywood, introducing global audiences to Nordic film talent. Sjöström, a pioneer in Swedish silent cinema, directed films such as the seminal *The Phantom Carriage* (1921), which were a major influence on later Nordic directors. Bridging generations of Swedish cinema, his memorable performance as the lead in Ingmar Bergman's *Wild Strawberries* (1957) remains one of the finest in the history of film.

Ingmar Bergman (1918–2007), one of the most influential filmmakers of the twentieth century, brought global attention to Swedish cinema with films like *The Seventh Seal* (1957) and *Persona* (1966), which examined themes of faith, isolation and mortality. His collaborations with actors such as Liv Ullmann (1938–) and Max von Sydow (1929–2020), and cinematographer Sven Nykvist (1922–2006), were instrumental to his development of a distinctive visual and narrative style.

Danish filmmaker Carl Theodor Dreyer (1889–1968) also left a strong mark with his films, such as *Day of Wrath* (1943) and *Ordet* (1955), noted for their measured pacing and exploration of profound religious themes.

Some contended that constant state intervention in the economy also hindered economic growth and artificially sustained unprofitable businesses and industries. The public sector became large and inefficient, while high taxes and the complex tax system encouraged tax evasion and even emigration. Famously, in 1976, the Swedish director Ingmar Bergman (1918–2007) was investigated on suspicion of tax evasion. Although the charges were later dropped, the ordeal led Bergman to leave Sweden for Munich, Germany, abandoning his unfinished projects and causing major financial losses to the Swedish film industry. He nevertheless later returned to Sweden and spent his last years on the island of Fårö, close to Gotland, in the Baltic Sea.

The more widespread criticism of social-democratic policies, however, came from the left. In the late 1960s, radical left-wing voices began demanding even more decisive measures to reduce social inequality, seeing state encouragement of economic growth not as a solution but as part of the problem. They wanted greater attention paid to gender equality, environmental issues, the dangers of nuclear energy and the failings of NATO and the United States. The social-democratic parties therefore found themselves in an awkward position: while presiding over record levels of economic growth and prosperity, they were nevertheless vulnerable to accusations that they had abandoned their ideological commitments and were content to merely manage capitalism, rather than reform it. The labor movement had become a part of the political establishment, its leaders increasingly alienated from grassroots concerns.

More serious cracks in the political consensus appeared in the first half of the 1970s, beginning with the 1973 oil crisis. The significantly increased fuel prices caused a halt in economic growth, which was followed by a downturn. Initially, attempts were made to manage the crisis by traditional state-managed measures, without fundamentally changing the system. Soon, however, cuts also needed to be considered, but scaling back the welfare state proved difficult—not least for the social democrats who had themselves been the architects of the welfare state. In fact, it was their inability to effectively mitigate the consequences of the crisis that in Denmark and Sweden caused the end of widespread popular support for the social democrats, who now faced increasing competition from the center-right.

In Sweden, bourgeois coalition governments were in power from 1976 to 1982 (led by Thorbjörn Fälldin, 1926–2016) and from 1991 to 1994 (led by Carl Bildt, 1949–). In Denmark, the Conservative People's Party (the successor of Højre), led by Poul Schlüter (1929–2021), held power from 1982 to 1993. From 1983 to 1986, Norway was governed by Høyre, led by Prime Minister Kåre Willoch (1928–2021), whose market liberal policies also influenced later Social Democratic governments. Thanks to its oil exports from the 1960s onward, Norway's economy weathered the oil crisis better than others.

The crisis also opened a space for new political forces to enter parliament. During the 1960s, a group of radical neoliberal critics of the welfare system had gained popularity, including Mogens Glistrup (1926–2008) in Denmark and Anders Lange (1904–74) in Norway. These voices strongly condemned high taxes, large self-serving bureaucracies and the stifling of individual initiative. Glistrup came to prominence in Denmark in 1971, when he revealed on television that he had not paid income tax on his substantial earnings. Instead of facing condemnation, he found significant public support, and Glistrup's party, the Progress Party (Fremskridtspartiet), won twenty-eight seats in the 1973 parliamentary elections. Norway experienced a similar "earthquake election" in the same year, with Anders Lange and three other representatives from his party entering the Storting.

By the 1980s, it had become clear that the challenges the Scandinavian welfare model had come to face were structural, requiring extensive economic and societal restructuring to overcome. Management of economic growth and wealth redistribution, once central to national policy, were overshadowed by emerging issues in the global economy that defied traditional state intervention. As environmental concerns grew, and globalization intensified competition for profits, unemployment rose significantly, peaking at 10–15 percent in the early 1990s. To many voters, far-reaching political change seemed inevitable and overdue.

THE MYSTERIOUS DEATH OF OLOF PALME

The murder of Sweden's Social Democratic prime minister Olof Palme (1927–86), which took place in central Stockholm in February 1986, was in some ways the symbolic end of the classic era of the Scandinavian welfare state. Palme was fatally wounded by a single gunshot while walking home with his wife, Lisbeth Palme, in central Stockholm. A second shot slightly wounded Lisbeth (1931–2018).

Committed to upholding and expanding the Swedish welfare state in Sweden, Olof Palme had been instrumental in developing his country's international reputation as the "conscience of the world," especially on peace and reconciliation issues. This was particularly notable during his first term as prime minister in 1969–76, when he famously and openly criticized the actions of the United States in the Vietnam War, resulting in a temporary freeze in US–Swedish relations. He was also a vocal opponent of apartheid in South Africa, a supporter of the anti-colonial struggles in Africa and the first Western head of government to visit Cuba after its revolution.

The assassination of Palme sent shock waves through Sweden and the international community. Despite multiple investigations and various theories about what had occurred, the murder remained unsolved, creating a lingering sense of unease and unresolved grief in Swedish society. In 2020, the investigation was finally closed, after thirty-four years, on the basis that a suspect had taken his own life in 2000. This decision faced widespread criticism, as the evidence for the suspect's guilt was circumstantial, and would have been legally too weak to ensure a trial had he still been alive.

19

EUROPEAN INTEGRATION AND POST–COLD WAR TRANSITION

IN WESTERN EUROPE, the economic growth that followed World War II coincided with the political will to take advantage of opportunities to liberalize international trade and decrease the likelihood of future wars by strengthening international economic ties. These ambitions were initially expressed by the European Coal and Steel Community (founded in 1951 by West Germany, France, Italy and the Benelux countries) and then by the European Economic Community (or EEC), which was founded in 1957 and in 1993 became the European Union (EU). The process of European integration, which was pivotal in shaping postwar European politics, initially saw only limited participation from the Scandinavian states. Over time, however, it proved to be a crucial vehicle for the Nordic region's post–Cold War transition.

In the Cold War era, Nordic countries needed access to Western European markets, but not all of them wished to be part of the EEC, which had resulted from the 1957 Treaty of

Rome. The Soviet Union regarded the EEC as a Western partisan alliance and an economic arm of NATO, which made membership awkward for states highly concerned about regional security. Of the Nordics, it was Finland that faced the most restrictions, and during its era of Finlandization it had to refrain from participation in any Western trading blocs.

The other Scandinavian states could at least join the European Free Trade Association (EFTA), which had been initiated by the United Kingdom to provide another option for countries that did not, or could not, join the EEC. In addition to the United Kingdom, the founding members, who signed the Stockholm Convention of 1960, were Austria, Denmark, Norway, Portugal, Sweden and Switzerland. EFTA was a success story, providing for its members a ten-year period of trade liberalization that led to the complete abolition of tariffs by 1970. Trade between the Scandinavian countries alone increased by over 200 percent between 1959 and 1967, and in 1961 it nearly matched the value of the region's trade with the EEC.

The year 1961 also saw the United Kingdom submit its first application for EEC membership. Denmark immediately followed suit, as its two main markets for agricultural exports were the United Kingdom and West Germany, which was already an EEC member. Denmark's application sparked a minor crisis in its relations with Sweden, which would have preferred the whole of EFTA to jointly negotiate an association agreement with the EEC. In 1962, Norway followed Denmark in submitting its own membership application. However, neither of these applications led anywhere, as the

United Kingdom's membership was vetoed by France, and Denmark and Norway refrained from pursuing theirs further.

In 1967, the United Kingdom, Norway and Denmark reapplied, but negotiations were again suspended due to a French veto. Danish prime minister Hilmar Baunsgaard (1920–89) subsequently proposed as an alternative the establishment of Nordek, an organization for Nordic economic cooperation that was to function similarly to EEC. A treaty was negotiated to establish the new organization, which was to be headquartered in Malmö, Sweden. But ultimately, Finland could not ratify the treaty due to the constraints of its sensitive relationship with the Soviet Union, and the plan fell through.

Danish prime minister Hilmar Baunsgaard, pictured here in 1971, advocated closer Nordic cooperation.

In the meantime, the negotiations of Denmark's and Norway's EEC membership applications resumed in 1970 and were concluded in 1972. In the same year, referendums were held in both countries on joining the EEC. Particularly in Norway, this issue became significantly contentious: all political forces that felt marginalized gathered under the anti-membership flag, resulting in 53.5 percent of the population voting against joining the EEC. For Norway, this meant that "the European issue" was effectively removed from the political agenda until the late 1980s.

In Denmark, where the agricultural sector supported joining, the result ended up being 63.3 percent in favor, and accession took place. However, just as with NATO, Denmark was a less than fully committed member of the EEC. In 1975, there was almost a new referendum on the question of continuing the membership, as there was a simultaneous danger of the United Kingdom leaving. A notably Euroskeptic political force was the Danish Social Democrats, which coupled with the non-socialist minority governments in the 1980s, leading to the so-called "footnote politics": footnotes had to be appended to agreements in Brussels to accommodate the opposition in the Danish parliament. In such contexts, Denmark liked to emphasize its Nordic identity, positioning itself as a bridge-builder between the EEC and the Nordic region. This helped to preserve Danish autonomy in relation to various kinds of European legislation.

In early 1986, the Social Democrats declared that they intended to vote against the *Single European Act*, which set the EEC an objective of establishing a single market by December 31, 1992 and codified European Political Cooperation, the forerunner of the European Union's Common Foreign and Security Policy. The Danish constitution required a referendum on any treaty that transferred significant sovereignty to international organizations, especially in the case of substantial political opposition. Another referendum was therefore in order, and 56.2 percent of Danish voters voted in favor of signing the *Single European Act*, a result largely caused by division in the social democratic electorate and low turnout on the "no" side.

Soon, however, the question of European integration came up again, now in the context of the end of the Cold War. The weakening and then disintegration of the Soviet Union meant significant changes in the regional security landscape: the Nordics were no longer the frontier states on the border between capitalism and communism, and potential opportunities arose for cooperation with partners on the other side of the Baltic Sea. The Nordic Balance, with its fundamental commitment not to upset the regional status quo, had become obsolete.

Scandinavia's global relationships also changed. In the welfare state era, the Nordics, especially Sweden, had branded themselves as promoters of peacefulness, democracy and solidarity with the developing world. But by the late 1980s and early 1990s, it was much less spectacular to be a peace-loving, neutral country. Indeed, after the demise of communism, what was there left to be neutral about?

At the same time, the Scandinavian welfare state model was in an increasingly deep crisis due to globalization and changes in the world economy. It was therefore felt—particularly by center-right politicians—that Scandinavia was in danger of being marginalized because of its non-functional welfare policies and loss of status in international politics.

It seemed that in a world emerging from the bipolar politics of the Cold War era, isolationism and cautiousness were no longer virtues. Instead, the ability to form networks and participate in them had become an asset. As the contours of the post–Cold War world were shaped, it was more advantageous to be active than passive.

One concrete way that the Nordics demonstrated their new international engagement was by extensively supporting the democratic, economic and social transition of the three Baltic states, which were now re-emerging after decades of Soviet occupation. Initially, this assistance differed little from traditional forms of Nordic overseas development aid and was aimed at supporting democratization. From the mid-1990s onward, however, Nordic efforts focused on assisting the Baltic states on their road to EU and NATO membership.

Another expression of the Nordics' new political direction was a significant shift in attitudes to the "European project." In October 1990, seven Danish parliamentary parties—including, significantly, the Social Democrats—agreed to a memorandum of changes to the Treaty of Rome that directed the EEC toward an increasingly political role, which the formerly Euroskeptic Denmark now appeared to support. The Maastricht Treaty, which laid the foundations for the European Union, was also backed by 125 Danish parliamentary votes, with just 30 votes against.

Several factors seem to have been important in this reorientation of Denmark's policy on Europe. Firstly, the unification of East and West Germany suggested the need for a more political approach to include the new Germany in the new

Europe. Secondly, the 1989 revolutions in the Eastern Bloc, and the fact that the European Commission (the executive institution of the EEC) seemed to be sympathetic toward the former Warsaw Pact states, had a very positive effect on the EEC's image in Denmark, especially among socialists. Finally, there was the prospect that the EEC would soon be significantly widened, as Austria had submitted its membership application in 1989, and, more crucially, Sweden submitted its own in 1991.

However, the first Danish referendum on the Maastricht Treaty, in June 1992, failed by a narrow majority, showing that the voters' opinion was different from that of the parliament. Again, one reason was the internal power struggle among Social Democrats, and another was a series of scandals surrounding the right-leaning Danish government. Subsequently, the terms of the Maastricht Treaty were renegotiated, and Denmark secured the right to opt out of four elements of the new organization: a single currency, common defense, EU citizenship and co-operation in aspects of justice and home affairs. These were then approved at a second referendum in Denmark, on May 18, 1993.

An even more unexpected case of newly found Euro-enthusiasm was Sweden, which during the Cold War had been adamant it would not seek accession to this "Western" bloc. The reasons behind Sweden's EEC/EU membership application are perhaps most emblematic of the changes that Scandinavia was going through in this period. By the early 1990s, the Swedish economy had started doing quite badly, with rising unemployment resulting in increased social spending. At the same time, the tax burden was already so heavy that putting up taxes further was politically unthinkable. Sweden's Social Democratic governments and social-democratic ideas were now held accountable for the country's persistent economic troubles. New outlooks and ideas were instead expected to come from center-right, non-socialist politicians, who had long advocated for Sweden's participation in the process of European integration. Trying to forestall electoral defeat, it was nevertheless the Social Democratic prime minister Ingvar Carlsson (1934–) who suddenly declared in autumn 1990 that the Swedish Social Democrats now supported Sweden's accession to the EU and would soon submit a membership application.

Sweden applied for membership in July 1991, with the approval of nearly all Swedish political and business elites, even if this sentiment was not completely shared by the Swedish public. Nevertheless, the Social Democrats were defeated in the 1991 parliamentary elections, and a right-wing coalition was elected, giving the conservative prime minister Carl Bildt the chance to start afresh in both domestic and foreign policy.

When Sweden announced its intention to apply for EU membership, it had consulted neither the Finns nor the Norwegians, and they were taken aback by the move. Nevertheless, both soon followed Sweden's example. For the overwhelmingly pro-European political and business elites in Finland, the question of EU membership initially remained connected to Finland's relationship with the Soviet Union. It seems that Finland's cautious president, Mauno Koivisto (1923–2017), only decided on the need for a Finnish EU application after the abortive hardline coup in Moscow in August

1991, three months before the formal disintegration of the Soviet Union.

For Finland, the prospect of joining the European Union represented a symbolic break with the era of Finlandization and, by facilitating Finland's reintegration into the West, a crucial, if indirect, security guarantee. In public, however, economic arguments were emphasized, which was appropriate, given that Finland was hit by deep recession and mass unemployment in the early 1990s, just as Sweden was.

Unlike Sweden and Finland, Norway already had its security provided through NATO, while North Sea oil and gas boosted its economy, giving it significant built-in resilience. Nonetheless, shortly after the Finnish move to seek EU membership, Norway, under Gro Harlem Brundtland's (1939–) Labour Party government, started its own negotiations for membership. In November 1992, the Norwegian parliament approved it, making Norway the last of the Nordic EFTA states to apply for EU membership in this period.

The accession negotiations of the three Nordic applicants and Austria were conducted in parallel, beginning in February 1993, with Norway joining the process in April. Although often viewed as a cohesive group, the Nordics mainly negotiated bilaterally. However, EU concessions given to one were usually extended to all. All four applicant governments committed to holding a domestic referendum on the outcome of the negotiations, which meant that the negotiators needed to consider the impact of policy positions and any eventual deal on the subsequent referendums, especially as there was strong domestic opposition to EU membership in Sweden and Norway.

Norwegian prime minister Gro Harlem Brundtland was a supporter of Norwegian EU membership during Norway's 1994 accession referendum.

For the Nordic countries, by far the most important aspects of the accession deal concerned four economic areas: the degree of agricultural transition; regional policy support; levels of budgetary contributions; and, for Norway, the protection of fisheries. In all these areas, the Nordic countries received relatively generous concessions. Subsidies to agriculture were expanded to include Arctic and sub-Arctic agriculture, and the European Union was to financially bear some of the costs of the transition. The European Union also agreed to provide extensive Structural Fund support, which aimed to reduce developmental disparities among EU members, especially for the border regions, and massive budgetary compensations.

On October 16, 1994, the first of the three accession referendums took place, with the Finns voting by a comfortable margin of 57 percent to 43 percent to enter the European Union on the negotiated terms. Sweden's referendum was held on November 13, 1994. With a record-high turnout, 52.2 percent of the electorate voted in favor and 46.9 percent against. The Norwegian referendum was held two weeks after Sweden's. Although Prime Minister Brundtland made much of the argument that staying out of the European Union would cut Norway off from its Nordic cousins, the result was a defeat: 47.8 percent for membership and 52.2 percent against. Again, the turnout was exceptionally high, at 88.9 percent.

Unlike in Sweden and Finland, in Norway Euroskeptics showed themselves undisturbed by recent changes in European politics, bringing together a mixture of economic self-interest (from farmers and public-sector employees), nationalist sentiment (especially from the older generation) and an intellectual critique of capitalism (particularly among younger people). Norway's comparatively more assured economic and security situation certainly played a role as well, as did the fact that it had already gained access to the European single market through membership of the European Economic Area (EEA), approved by the Nowegian parliament in October 1992.

Iceland, with its strong fisheries interests, remained most cautious of all, with even the EEA agreement encountering strong opposition, and eventually passing the Icelandic parliament by a margin of thirty-three votes to twenty-three, only after some government coercion.

By the mid-1990s, Denmark was no longer the only Nordic member of the European Union, but in 1994 the result was continued political fragmentation. While Sweden and Finland became members of the European Union on January 1, 1995, Iceland and Norway decided to stay outside it.

CONTINUING SCANDINAVIAN EUROSKEPTICISM

In some ways, Scandinavians have continued to be reluctant Europeans, rejecting closer ties with the European Union on several further occasions. On September 28, 2000, Denmark held a referendum on adopting the euro, which was rejected by 53.1 percent of voters on a high turnout of 87.5 percent. The pro-euro campaign warned of job losses and diminished influence outside the eurozone, while the anti-euro side emphasized threats to Danish democracy, sovereignty and identity, portraying the euro as a step toward EU federalism and increased immigration.

Similarly, on September 14, 2003, Sweden rejected the euro, with 55.9 percent voting against it on an 81 percent turnout. The decisive factors were skepticism about the promised economic benefits and the belief that it would be possible to adopt the euro later if needed. In particular, the "no" side argued that the Swedish economy was performing well compared to many eurozone countries, making a transition to the euro seem unnecessary.

Euroskepticism has also been embraced by Scandinavian right-wing populist parties opposing EU moves toward federalism and liberal immigration policies, and instead promising to defend national culture and the Nordic welfare model. However, most Nordic voters do not vote for Euroskeptic parties, and the positions of the latter have become more moderate over time, especially after the United Kingdom's Brexit vote in 2016.

Interestingly, Scandinavia's relative reluctance to further European integration has been accompanied by a very high degree of compliance with EU legislation and regulation by Nordic EU and EEA member states. Even the two non-members, Norway and Iceland, participate fully in EU market integration and research cooperation, with the notable exceptions of the agricultural and fisheries sectors.

20

POLITICAL DEVELOPMENTS IN THE 1990s AND 2000s

AFTER THE END OF THE COLD WAR, the Nordics gradually shed their exceptionalism in favor of some form of European normalcy. Yet the region did not entirely give up the unique character it had developed in previous decades. The relative decline of the welfare state continued, but it never led to a complete collapse. Immigration became an increasingly contentious political issue and facilitated the rise of right-wing populist parties, but the Nordics have nevertheless remained internationally renowned for their commitment to liberal values and humanitarianism.

Sweden's center-right government of Carl Bildt (in power from 1991 to 1994) introduced harsh retrenchment cuts to the welfare state system and a variety of other reforms, including privatization of state-owned enterprises, lowering of taxes, and preparations for Sweden's EU membership. At the same time, prices of goods and services in Sweden rose rapidly, property prices fell and unemployment reached record levels, meaning that many of these measures had the character of crisis management rather than a thought-out political program. It was arguably during the Bildt cabinet that the Swedish public began to associate center-right governments with economic downturns and austerity measures. In the 1994 elections, the Social Democrats, led by Ingvar Carlsson, were returned to power. Göran Persson (1949–) was finance minister and would later succeed Carlsson as prime minister after the 1996 elections.

In 2006, however, another center-right coalition, led by Fredrik Reinfeldt (1965–), won the general elections, marking a notable shift once again. With new vigor, Reinfeldt's government pursued market-oriented reforms with tax cuts, deregulation and privatization, but Sweden's generous welfare provision nevertheless survived, if to a more modest extent. Despite initial skepticism, Reinfeldt's coalition achieved reelection in 2010. By that point, the economy and the welfare state were no longer the only issues on the political agenda. Instead, the challenges associated with immigration had emerged as a central political issue, dividing the whole region.

During the boom years after World War II, Scandinavia had seen significant labor immigration, mostly from adjacent countries such as Finland at first, but later from Turkey, Yugoslavia and other Southern European states. Initially, immigration was mostly unproblematic and managed as a labor-market issue—in the 1960s, Swedish companies even had recruitment programs in places such as Greece and Italy. After the onset of the economic downturn in the early 1970s, labor migration was halted, but it soon gave way to other kinds of migration, including secondary immigration (the reunification of families) and asylum seekers. Due to being signatories to international refugee and humanitarian conventions, and more fundamentally because of the liberal values shared across the political spectrum, the Scandinavian states could do little to stop it. At the same time, their generous and universalist welfare systems ensured their attractiveness as a destination.

Starting from the mid-1980s, as the number of war refugees went up, Scandinavia's hitherto liberal immigration laws gradually began to be tightened. Nevertheless, far-right movements found in immigration a political weapon against mainstream parties that were unable or unwilling to address the issue. More than simple racism or xenophobia, welfare chauvinism has been the most salient component in this anti-immigration discourse: the idea that for reasons of education or culture, immigrants would not, or could not, become productive, contributing citizens, but would instead remain a burden on the public purse. Eventually, right-wing populist parties making use of this rhetoric would gain seats in all Scandinavian parliaments.

Norway was perhaps least susceptible to right-wing populism, thanks to its economic resilience. By the 1980s, the oil industry had become the country's main source of income, through both taxes and excise duties, as well as through direct sales of oil and gas by the state. Other areas related to the oil sector, including logistics and research and development, also developed rapidly. Yet crisis eventually struck even Norway. In the 1980s (circa 1983–87), the oil dollars brought about the so-called "Jappetiden" (from the English word "yuppie"), an economic bubble that ended with a banking crisis and the devaluation of the Norwegian currency, as the price of oil fell in 1986, reducing state revenues. This caused a wave of bankruptcies in 1988–89, because a considerable number of Norwegian companies had become directly or indirectly over-dependent on oil prices.

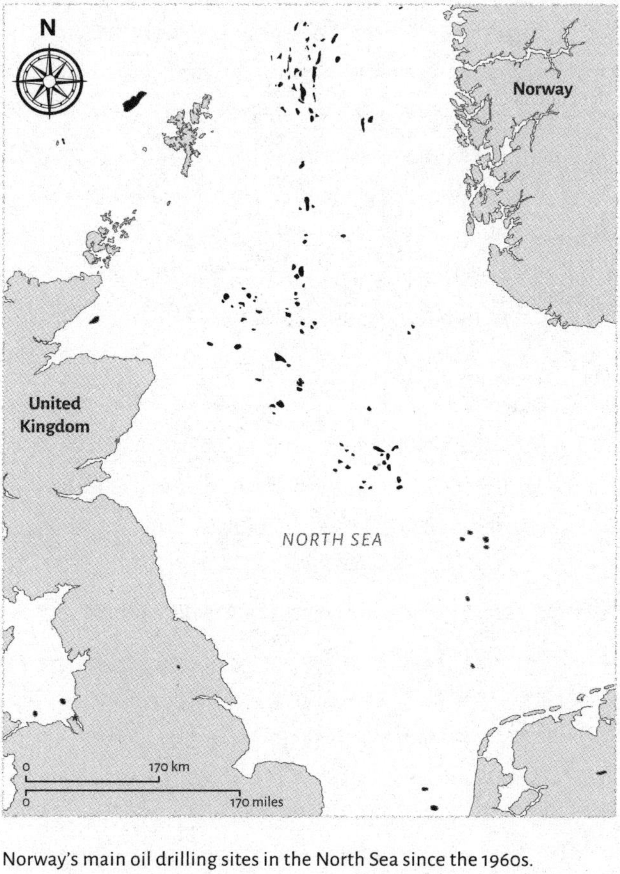

Norway's main oil drilling sites in the North Sea since the 1960s.

ENVIRONMENTALISM AND ENERGY POLICIES

Nordic countries are widely recognized as global leaders in environmentalism. They consistently rank among the world's most sustainable nations, with particularly ambitious environmental goals. Sustainability has also become a major part of how the Nordics promote themselves in international contexts.

Rooted in the nineteenth-century movements for sustainable forest management and national parks, Scandinavian environmentalism initially focused on conserving natural ecosystems. In the twentieth century and even more so in the twenty-first century, however, it gradually encompassed an ever-broader set of environmental concerns. Beginning in the early 1970s, the Nordic countries were some of the first to establish ministries for the environment, and in the 1980s among the first to see the rise of Green parties.

Particularly important have been the ways in which Nordic environmental movements intersected with national energy debates. Following the 1973 oil crisis, Denmark investigated nuclear energy as an alternative energy source, but experienced significant public resistance, which ultimately led the Danish parliament in the mid-1980s to formally abandon the country's nuclear energy plans and to prioritize the development of renewable energy sources instead. Meanwhile, Sweden had started investing in nuclear power in the 1950s, with nuclear energy meeting nearly half of its electricity needs by the 1980s. However, at a 1980 referendum, a majority opted to phase out nuclear power—a decision that was reinforced by public concerns after the 1986 Chernobyl disaster in the Soviet Union.

In the decades that followed, the Nordic countries have come to widely embrace and promote the so-called ecological modernization framework:

the idea that technological advancements make it possible to achieve ambitious environmental goals and economic growth at the same time. A major step toward its adoption was the 1987 *Our Common Future* report, led by Norway's Gro Harlem Brundtland, which advocated for environmentally conscious economic policies and the concept of sustainability. This resulted in a near-universal commitment to "green growth" across the Nordic region, with each country implementing strict environmental policies aimed at reducing carbon emissions and promoting renewable energy sources. From 1990 to 2011, these policies enabled Nordic countries to increase their GDP by 55 percent while reducing greenhouse gas emissions by 9 percent.

Although different Scandinavian countries have prioritized different alternative energy resources—hydropower in Norway and Sweden, geothermal energy in Iceland and wind power in Denmark—they have also coordinated their efforts to create a unified energy strategy. The integrated Scandinavian electricity market, supported by transmission cables linking the countries to one another, makes it possible, for example, for surplus hydropower from Norway and Sweden to flow to Denmark, while surplus wind power from Denmark can at other times supply Norway and Sweden, maintaining a balance across the grid.

Today, environmental consciousness in the Nordics has shifted from its activist roots to broad-based social participation. Ecological awareness is interwoven into Nordic identity, with green policies backed by multiple political parties. But while Scandinavian environmentalism has continued to emphasize balanced growth, the emergence of radical "degrowth" movements, with activists such as Sweden's Greta Thunberg (2003–) at the helm, has sparked a new debate over whether to seek solutions within established systems or change them through transformative environmental action.

In the following period, from the late 1980s to the early 2000s, Norway experienced constant political shifts. Gro Harlem Brundtland's social democratic Labour government of 1986–89 was replaced by the center-right government of Jan P. Syse (1930–97), which soon collapsed due to internal divisions over "the European issue." Brundtland returned to power in 1990 but failed to achieve her main goal, Norway's membership of the European Union. Labour remained in power, led by Thorbjørn Jagland (1950–), but economic instability persisted until the latter half of the 1990s, and in 1997, a right-wing coalition of smaller parties took power, marking the first time since 1933 that neither of the two largest parties—Labour and the Conservatives—participated in the government.

Outside of EU membership, it was the funding of the welfare state, particularly health care, that remained the contentious issue in this period. Subsequent governments also faced increasing challenges over environmental concerns, especially in connection to Norway's continued oil exploration. Jens Stoltenberg's (1959–) left-wing government, in power from 2005, successfully navigated the global economic crisis, partly thanks to Norway's historical oil revenues, but faced much criticism from the left over its environmental policies. It was nevertheless re-elected in 2009.

In July 2011, Norway was devastated by an unprecedented act of mass murder, committed by a right-wing extremist, Anders Behring Breivik (1979–). Breivik first set off a bomb in Oslo, killing eight people and injuring thirty, and then engaged in a shooting spree at a Labour Party youth summer camp on the island of Utøya, close to Oslo. Apparently wanting to take revenge on the party for its pro-immigration stance, Breivik killed a further sixty-nine people, most of them teenagers, and injured sixty-six others. He was arrested and subsequently tried, declared sane and found guilty. In August 2012, Breivik was sentenced to a minimum of twenty-one years in prison. The response of the Norwegian political elites and the public to Breivik's murderous actions was one of unity and the reaffirmation of humanitarian and liberal democratic values. However, survivors questioned whether Norway had done enough to deal with the threat of the right-wing extremist ideology that had motivated him.

Denmark had a series of coalition governments, led by Conservative prime minister Poul Schlüter, which were in power from 1982 to 1993, after the Social Democrats had seemingly exhausted their ability to lead the country out of crisis. Over time, Schlüter's four-party coalition was replaced by a coalition of three parties and then two. As demonstrated by this remarkable electoral success, the crisis measures the government implemented were fairly effective at strengthening the currency, stimulating the labor market and reducing foreign debt. In January 1993, the Schlüter government was forced to resign due to justice minister Erik Ninn-Hansen's (1922–2014) so-called "Tamil scandal": Ninn-Hansen had issued a decree prohibiting Tamil war refugees from inviting their family members to Denmark, which was not in line with existing law.

Poul Nyrup Rasmussen (1943–), leading a left-wing coalition, became the next prime minister and remained in power until 2001. Rasmussen's government managed to further stimulate the labor market through expansive economic policies, but the slow decline of the welfare state nevertheless continued. In November 2001, elections led to a right-wing coalition government headed by Anders Fogh Rasmussen (1953–). His campaign focused on tax cuts and labor-market reforms, aimed at stimulating growth and competitiveness. More controversially, he also campaigned for the tightening of immigration rules, reflecting broader debates about multiculturalism and Danish identity. Despite criticisms, Rasmussen's coalition managed to maintain power through successive elections.

The aftermath of the 2001 elections was also when the far-right Danish People's Party gained substantial influence, becoming the third-largest party in parliament. Subsequently, immigration remained a central political issue. In 2002, Denmark significantly tightened its immigration legislation, making it among the most restrictive in Europe. From 2005 to 2006, Denmark also experienced the so-called "Muhammad cartoons controversy," when cartoons of the prophet Muhammad printed in a Danish newspaper sparked widespread anti-Danish protests and exposed the Danish government's ineptness at handling cultural sensitivities around immigration. Thereafter, Denmark's immigration rules grew even more restrictive, raising the bar for access to permanent residency and citizenship, and limiting recent immigrants' rights to social welfare benefits.

In terms of security policy, it was Finland and Sweden that went through the most significant development arc. Having given up their claims to neutrality upon applying for EU membership, both remained formally non-aligned, yet sought relationships with NATO through membership in its Partnership for Peace (PfP) program. Another security provider of importance was the European Union. The Maastricht Treaty included a commitment to develop a common foreign and security policy leading to a common defense policy (CSDP), which foresaw mutual assistance among EU member states should one of them fall victim to armed aggression.

Sweden and Finland came to contribute proactively to the CSDP, while Denmark had secured the right to opt out from its military aspects. Interestingly, Norway, too, eventually became quite proactively involved in CSDP operations, as well as in the dealings of the European Defence Agency (EDA). Norway was arguably incentivized to engage in EU-related security and defense matters to increase its visibility and be perceived as an international player. Norwegian defense expenditure also remained the highest in Scandinavia.

Finland and Sweden, which unlike most EU member states were in the same position vis-a-vis NATO, also sought ways to become security innovators, shifting away from the essentially reactive disposition of the Cold War era. In 1996, Sweden and Finland made an innovative joint proposal for strengthening the European Union's crisis management capability, and subsequently participated quite extensively in crisis management initiatives under both the EU and NATO flags, using both military and non-military instruments. For instance, in 2007 Finland participated in a multinational rapid-reaction EU "battle group," together with Germany and the Netherlands, and a "Nordic battle group" was launched in 2008 with Finnish,

Swedish, Norwegian, Estonian and Irish troops. The task of these units was to provide humanitarian support and to perform search, rescue and evacuation duties.

The question of joining NATO also came up. In 2003, the leaders of the Swedish and Danish conservatives, Carl Bildt and Uffe Ellemann-Jensen (1941–2022), issued a joint statement arguing that Finland and Sweden should join NATO or risk losing their influence in European security discussions. Yet domestic support for Finnish and Swedish NATO membership remained insufficient in the 1990s, 2000s and 2010s, meaning that they had to rely on alternative instruments such as the PfP, and then its inner circle, NATO's Enhanced Opportunities Partners, which both Finland and Sweden joined in 2014.

The new focus on "troubleshoot security" was to the detriment of the earlier emphasis on territorial defense, especially for Sweden. In 2004, a new defense bill by the Swedish Social Democratic minority government stated that Sweden no longer perceived any serious threats to its territorial security. Consequently, one third of its military forces were disbanded, its defense staff reduced by one quarter and its fleets of submarines and fighter aircraft substantially reduced, marking the end of Sweden's Cold War–era policy of armed neutrality. In Finland, by contrast, adherence to the territorial defense strategy remained a central policy objective, and it consistently regarded Russia as a strategic security threat. Finland therefore preserved substantial defensive capabilities in addition to crisis management and expeditionary operations.

Danish security policy proved to be more "Atlanticist" than that of others, with Denmark promptly and repeatedly siding with the United States during the latter's global "war on terror," even if there was a broader European—not to mention Nordic—reluctance to do so. Denmark provided troops during the US invasion of Iraq in 2003, but also participated in UN peacekeeping operations and NATO-led air strikes against Serbia in 1999.

The 2014 Russian annexation of Crimea and invasion of Ukraine proved, in some ways, to be a wake-up call, leading to the reversal of the Nordics', and particularly Sweden's, long decline in military readiness. Defense expenditure began to recover, indicating that the worsening regional security environment could lead the Nordic countries to rethink some aspects of the Cold War–era Scandinavian exceptionalism that still lingered.

THE SÁMI INDIGENOUS MINORITY

In recent decades, the Sámi people have seen a resurgence of cultural and political activism. The Sámi are the indigenous inhabitants of northern Scandinavia. Their traditional settlement area, approximately 149,942 square miles (388,350 square kilometers), spans four states: Norway, Sweden, Finland and Russia's Kola Peninsula. Today, up to 50,000 Sámi live in Norway, approximately 17,000 in Sweden, 6,000 in Finland and 2,000 in Russia.

In Sweden and Finland, the Sámi are recognized as both an indigenous people and a national minority, while in Norway they hold the status of indigenous people. Unique to Norway and Sweden, reindeer husbandry is a right reserved exclusively for the Sámi minority.

The establishment of the Sámi Parliament (Sámediggi, in the Northern Sámi language) in 1989 marked a significant step toward Sámi self-governance. The legislative body aims to safeguard and promote Sámi rights, culture and language, providing a platform for addressing issues pertinent to Sámi communities. By 2004, the eighteenth Sámi Conference declared the Sámi as one people with a shared history, language, culture, traditions, social life and vision for the future, despite the national borders dividing them.

The conference also highlighted that the states of Norway, Sweden, Finland and Russia have been partially established on territories traditionally belonging to the Sámi. The forceful assimilationist policies that were exercised by these states for over a century have had deep socio-psychological impacts on Sámi communities, with many of their members finding it hard to share their personal or family experiences of being prevented from speaking their native language or shamed for their traditional nomadic lifestyle.

21

NORDIC CULTURAL EXPORTS AND "SCANDIMANIA"

WHILE SCANDINAVIAN COUNTRIES HAVE increasingly come to resemble other European nations in their domestic and foreign policies, they have also been able to successfully capitalize on aspects of their history and culture that convey positive images of Nordicness to global audiences. Some of this can be characterized as "nation-branding" or "region-branding," a form of deliberate soft power projection aimed at attracting consumer and investor interest. However, only a small portion of this activity is deliberate. Arguably, everyone has a brand—whether they are aware of it or not—and the Nordic brand has been very successful, even without conscious strategic promotion.

Nordic cultural exports are deeply intertwined with features specifically associated with the Nordic countries. These include their peripheral—and therefore exotic—geographical location, their "untouched" nature, their unique history and culture, and more. In hindsight, the twentieth century's decades of innovative domestic politics and multifaceted internationalism probably prepared Scandinavian countries particularly well for the role of major cultural exporters. Their appeal is drawn from their relatively low levels of military tension after World War II, a social model that is poised between socialism and capitalism, and the liberal, progressive and enlightened tone of Nordic societies. Scandinavian cultural exports are therefore easily associated with positive values such as peacefulness, egalitarianism, solidarity, gender equality and environmentalism. There are many examples, and this short chapter will mention only a few of them.

The Vikings remain a source of international fascination, and one of the most recognized tropes of Nordicness, familiar from forms of popular entertainment such as film and television, young-adult fiction, music and computer games. This fascination is not new. In the beginning of the nineteenth century, the pirates of the north came to symbolize a different, more primitive and raw form of Europeanness that appealed to European nations of Germanic origin who were looking for their own roots. For German composers such as Richard Wagner, who drew inspiration from early Germanic legends preserved in Icelandic poetry, and for Victorian British gentlemen translating Old Norse sagas into English, the Vikings were not a barbarian menace but provided a glimpse into an alternative and supposedly more genuine European past, untouched by Christianity. Similar attitudes to Vikings continue today—and not only in innocent ways, as is demonstrated by the appropriation of Norse imagery by much of the contemporary European far right.

A very different example of a successful Nordic cultural export are the Nobel Prizes—the preeminent global awards recognizing achievement in many fields, hosted and awarded yearly by award committees in Sweden and Norway. Established by the Swedish nineteenth-century inventor Alfred Nobel, they have contributed to the success of many writers, public figures and scientists—not least Scandinavian ones, such as the Danish physicist Niels Bohr (1885–1962), who in the early twentieth century made groundbreaking contributions to atomic structure and quantum theory. The Nobel Prizes' reputation rests not only on longevity (they were established in the late nineteenth century), but also on the idea that peaceful innovation is something specifically Nordic. Nobel, the inventor of dynamite, accomplished a brilliant public relations move by funding, among other prizes, an international peace prize, which is awarded by the Norwegian Nobel Committee. But the peace prize would hardly be so prestigious if it weren't for Scandinavia's reputation for peacefulness and benevolent neutrality—whether justified or not—which most countries would find difficult to emulate. This reputation has also helped to sideline the question of why small circles of Swedish experts (and Norwegian experts, in the case of the peace prize) should have the right to decide who is worthy of receiving the most prestigious awards in the world.

Some Nordic cultural exports first saw success in the early-to-mid-twentieth century, and therefore have an even stronger association with Scandinavia's progressive values. The children's books of the Swedish author Astrid Lindgren (1907–2002) are a good example: relatively little known in the English-speaking world, with the exception of the Pippi Longstocking series, they have had a major, formative influence on generations of children across Northern, Eastern and Central Europe. In some ways a continuation of the earlier tradition of Swedish children's literature established by authors such as Selma Lagerlöf (1858–1940) and Elsa Beskow (1874–1953), Lindgren's books, including those about Pippi Longstocking and Emil of Lönneberga, were a breath of fresh air for a genre often characterized by stilted didacticism. Themes such as children's rights, social and gender equality and compassion for the poor are woven into Lindgren's stories through humor and adventure in a way that has appealed to readers far beyond Sweden. Of course, there are also other examples of successful Nordic children's authors. One might mention, for instance, the famous Finnish writer Tove Jansson's (1914–2001) stories about the Moomins, which often deal with rather dark topics such as loneliness, fear and survival in harsh natural conditions, but also convey soothing images of domesticity and family support in the face of uncertainty and danger.

Nordic architecture design is undoubtedly another twentieth-century success. Globally recognizable, and having produced such renowned mid-century figures as Alvar Aalto (1898–1976), Arne Jacobsen (1902–71) and Hans Wegner (1914–2007), it is characterized by simplicity and understatement, the use of natural materials and the maximization of natural light whenever possible. Its mantra of functionality over aesthetics—which makes outward beauty but a component in an overall package promoting well-being and good quality

THE ABBA PHENOMENON

With its name derived from the initials of its members' first names, ABBA was formed in Sweden in 1972 by Agnetha Fältskog (1950–), Björn Ulvaeus (1945–), Benny Andersson (1946–) and Anni-Frid Lyngstad (1945–). It remains one of the most popular pop groups in the world.

ABBA first rose to international fame after winning the Eurovision Song Contest in 1974 with "Waterloo." This victory marked Sweden's first win at the contest and launched the group onto the global stage, which it capitalized on with a series of worldwide hits in the 1970s, including "Dancing Queen," "Mamma Mia" and "Take a Chance on Me." Known for blending influences from pop, rock and disco, and intricate harmonies and polished production, ABBA's songs have continued to appeal to generations of audiences, particularly in Europe, North America and Australia. ABBA's stage costumes and choreographed performances have likewise become instantly recognizable, adding to their iconic status.

After a split in 1982, ABBA's music gained new momentum with the release of *ABBA Gold* in 1992, which remains one of the best-selling compilation albums to date. The debut of *Mamma Mia!* as a stage musical in 1999 and its film adaptation in 2008 introduced ABBA's music to yet another generation, further cementing its legacy. The 2022 launch of ABBA Voyage, a hologram concert performance in London, has been another great success, highlighting their continued cultural relevance.

of life—can be traced back to interwar-era experiments with rationalizing Scandinavian domestic life, which continued after World War II. Democratized by international companies such as the famous furniture retailer IKEA, founded in 1943, Nordic design has had a far-reaching influence, as have closely related fields such as architecture and planning. Today, they also integrate modern Nordic values, such as sustainability and environmentalism.

The "New Nordic Food" culinary movement, originating in the early 2000s, is an example of a more recent, and hugely successful, Scandinavian cultural export that also emphasizes simplicity and sustainability. It aims to anchor food preparation and consumption in the local environment and traditions, putting strong emphasis on seasonality and high-quality local ingredients. Many chefs and restaurants that have adopted these principles have gained global renown, and the movement has influenced other cuisines around the globe. However, the prominence of the New Nordic Food as a kind of ideology may create the misleading impression that most Scandinavians eat this way, which is of course not the case.

A perhaps somewhat unexpected cultural export has been crime literature, sometimes referred to as Nordic noir, which has spilled over into other mediums such as film and television. Although there were some early successes in the 1960s and 1970s, such as the Swedish authors Maj Sjöwall (1935–2020) and Per Wahlöö's (1926–75) novels about police detective Martin Beck, Nordic crime literature experienced a veritable boom in the 2000s and 2010s, making such writers as Henning Mankell (1948–2015), Stieg Larsson (1954–2004) and Jo

Nesbø (1960–) world-famous. This might seem strange, given that twentieth-century Scandinavia has been known for its historically low crime rates (Iceland's are almost nonexistent), a high perception of public safety, generous penal policies and generally lenient attitudes toward most types of crime. Perhaps it is exactly this lack of crime and overall feeling of safety that has helped to make fictional depictions of crime in the Nordic region all the more striking. Both domestic and international audiences have been fascinated by stories revealing possible cracks in the edifice of supposedly perfect Scandinavian societies, perhaps exposing dark forces hiding underneath. Writers have certainly met this demand. Nordic crime novels are known for their engagement with social problems and challenges, as well as the psychology and personal failings of their brilliant but often imperfect detective figures.

Finally, but certainly not least interestingly, we have self-help books and related genres that have tried to capture the specifically Scandinavian way of life, highlighting cultural stereotypes that supposedly express some intangible truth about what it really means to be Nordic. Perhaps the most-promoted example of these has been *hygge*—a Danish or Norwegian concept expressing the idea of comfort, contentment and cosiness—which has been the subject of countless books, websites and merchandise. *Sisu*, the Finnish word for grit or resilience, is another well-known idea, and the Swedish term *lagom*, meaning something like "just right," is another example. Whether there is, in fact, anything particularly unique or even untranslatable about these concepts remains open to debate, but the wish and readiness to look for a key to the

Nordic way of life is in itself telling, and a testimony to the global cultural appeal of Scandinavia. Sometimes referred to as "Scandimania," this international fascination with Scandinavia has changed over time, but at present it seems unlikely to abate, finding expression in a continuous stream of old and new images of Nordicness.

22

SCANDINAVIAN SUCCESSES AND FAILURES

AS WE HAVE SEEN, the Nordic region is a vast expanse of land, rich in all kinds of natural features, yet for the most part—outside of the major urban centers, which themselves are a comparatively recent addition to the Nordic landscapes—it is sparsely populated. Nordic history can be described as a series of attempts by humans to survive and succeed in an often unwelcoming world, meeting challenges that have ranged from volcanic activity and climate fluctuations to war and pandemics. Scandinavians have not been passive spectators: they have actively shaped their own history and have had a considerable impact on European and global history as well—be it through Scandinavian expansionism in the Viking Age, the championship of Lutheran Protestantism in the early modern period, or the development of the Nordic welfare state in the twentieth century.

The earliest millennia of human settlement in Scandinavia very much underscore its peripheral status relative to Europe's cultural and economic core in the south. With most of its lands badly suited to the agriculture that was possible at the time, Scandinavia became a meeting zone between settled and nomadic lifestyles, with the indigenous Sámi people gradually pushed northward as farming techniques improved. Some of the original difference between rich agricultural Denmark in the south, with its European trade and direct openness to foreign cultural impulses, and the wild north still stands today. The mysteriousness of Nordic nature continues to capture our imagination just as much as—if not more than—the *hygge* of the Scandinavian capitals and small towns.

For most of its early history, Scandinavia was also peripheral, from the European vantage point, in terms of what it had to trade—originally it was mostly luxury goods, such as furs and walrus ivory—and what it could teach, in terms of ideas and innovation. For Scandinavians, the precarity of their existence encouraged a flatter societal structure, with less class differentiation and more gender equality than elsewhere. More elaborate social hierarchies tended to appear in times of warmer climate, better trade and more wealth—only to wane again when these conditions reversed.

It was the Viking Age, with its raids, trade and settler colonialism, that rudely pushed Scandinavia into the center of European awareness. The pacification of these militant pagans of the north took centuries, and, in the end, the problem did not have a military solution. Instead, gradual and voluntary Christianization, along with the wealth amassed in the Viking Age, helped to kickstart the successful development of European-style kingdoms in Scandinavia. Going forward, these remained mostly concerned with succession struggles and conflicts with each other, and no longer presented an acute threat to the rich countries of Western Europe. At the same time, Scandinavia managed to avoid the fate that befell some other parts of the Baltic Sea region, which were targeted by medieval crusades and Christianization by force, leading to foreign dominance and serfdom of the native population.

Well-managed Christianization also opened the door to the political consolidation and further development of the medieval kingdoms of Denmark, Norway and Sweden. But the late medieval period, with its cooling climate, the Black Death pandemic and a multitude of knock-on effects, proved to be a difficult time for Scandinavia, as it was for much of Europe. A semi-successful attempt to unite all three Scandinavian kingdoms under the same monarch, known as the Kalmar Union, was plagued by wars and ultimately failed in the early sixteenth century, with Sweden breaking away. Reformation and its military successes gave proto-absolutist Sweden a strong head start in the early modern period that followed. Norway, however, fared much worse, losing its independence for centuries.

The sixteenth and seventeenth centuries were the most warlike time in the history of Sweden and Denmark, as they competed over resources and political hegemony. Largely due to the demands of this constant war-making, Sweden and Denmark developed into highly effective bureaucratic and militaristic states, which allowed them to have an outsized military and political impact, relative to their size and population. In the end, however, the imperial adventurism proved to be an expensive failure. After the Great Northern War in the early eighteenth century, both were again reduced to being second-rate players in European politics.

The eighteenth century that followed was largely a time of peaceful economic development, but it was also a time of internal turmoil, as the ideas of Enlightenment gained a foothold even in the north. Absolutism, which had developed in the second half of the seventeenth century, was increasingly beleaguered in both Sweden and Denmark as demands for greater political and personal freedoms increased. This was also a period during which the Scandinavian kingdoms dabbled in state-led colonial expansion and domestic economic interventionism, but neither proved sustainable for long.

Still, the imperial dreams persisted, and delusions of their own grandeur can be blamed for dragging Sweden and Denmark into the Napoleonic Wars. This was a very expensive failure, which for Sweden ultimately resulted in the forced abdication of its king and the loss of a third of its territory—the whole of Finland—to Russia. Denmark, which eventually ended up on the wrong side (that of Napoleon), was for its part forced to cede the whole of Norway to Sweden. Yet Norway was never happy with Swedish rule, which ultimately made the union a failure. The countries that gained the most during this period of turmoil were Norway and Finland, who were able to make use of changing times to create some important institutional preconditions for their future independence.

The onward march of the new modernizing ideologies, especially romantic nationalism and liberalism, affected the whole of Scandinavia in the nineteenth century, undermining the power of the crown and investing it in each nation instead—and even in the community of Scandinavian nations. Over time, the old conservative kingdoms of Sweden and Denmark were pushed toward modernizing their constitutions, adopting the principle of government accountability to the parliament and instituting universal suffrage. But until this all could happen, outdated political structures created strong tensions in the societies that were rapidly changing due to industrialization. In the end, these challenges were overcome peacefully for the most part: a testament to the core resilience of Scandinavian societies. A particularly important success story was the secession of Norway from Sweden: the first bloodless, non-coercive secession of a state in European history.

New popular movements and ideologies that affected Scandinavian politics in the late nineteenth and early twentieth century—such as the women's and labor movements—achieved just about the right amount of early success so as not to radicalize but instead to focus on peaceful development in a reformist fashion. For the labor movement in particular, the early decades of the twentieth century were a crucial time for the development of its "Goldilocks" balance: a movement that was strong, but not overwhelmingly strong, and therefore had to appeal not just to urban workers but also to other groups in society. To do that, it adopted, from the first half of the 1930s onward, a broad national unity perspective that set the scene for the social democrats' continued postwar electoral success.

After their successful neutrality in World War I and avoidance of a postwar revolution or civil war (Finland being an exception), the Scandinavian states had gained much self-confidence. Yet World War II was, in many ways, a major reality check. Early in the war, Denmark and Norway were occupied by Nazi Germany, making it clear that neutrality was no guarantee of security. Finland was in an even more difficult situation, fighting two bloody wars against the Soviet Union. And even Greenland, the Faroe Islands and Iceland ended up being occupied during the war, if only by the Allies. Sweden was the only Scandinavian country that remained successfully neutral, but the pressure placed on it by Nazi Germany meant that it had to go along with some morally dubious demands to accommodate German interests.

Thanks to having been left alone and intact, Sweden was best placed to capitalize on the postwar period of prolonged economic growth, but its neighbors soon caught up. Crucially, the social democrats entered a long period of electoral dominance and could now start fully realizing their ambitious social-welfare plans in the tradition of political consensus-building. Importantly, the "workfare" ethic of universalist social-welfare provision "from cradle to grave" created not just an opportunity for citizens to benefit but also the expectation that they would contribute. This philosophy also led Scandinavia down a darker path, involving forced sterilizations of people seen as not "productive enough," a moral failure largely concealed by the overall success story of the Nordic welfare state.

During the Cold War period, the quality of life in Scandinavia rose to heights unknown almost anywhere in the world. At the same time, the "Nordic Balance" security configuration in the Baltic Sea area meant that international tensions remained low, even as meaningful policy choices on regional security were severely constrained by the overwhelming threat of the Soviet Union. To compensate, the Scandinavian countries developed their own small-state internationalist identity as bridge-builders between the East and the West, engaging particularly with the developing world—but also turning a blind eye to human rights abuses in the Soviet Union.

The end of the Cold War was in many ways a breaking point for Scandinavia: structural changes in the world economy had undermined its high-tax, high-spend welfare state, and the fall of the USSR had made the Nordic Balance obsolete. Looking for a new identity in a changing world, Finland and Sweden decided to join the process of European integration, as Denmark had already done in the early 1970s.

But in the end, the Nordic brand proved more resilient and successful than many had feared, not least culturally. Even in a globalized and predominantly neoliberal environment, Scandinavia's consensus-oriented political culture did not let it down. This success made it an attractive destination for immigration of all kinds, something that the Scandinavian states have not always proven themselves well-equipped to handle.

Today, more challenges have arrived. Russia's military aggression against its neighboring states, which began in 2008, has proven that any post–Cold War hopes for a permanent relaxation of international tensions in regional proximity were unfounded. This point became even more obvious after the beginning of full-scale war in February 2022, when both Sweden and Finland applied for NATO membership, creating, for the first time, security policy unity across the Nordic region. It remains to be seen whether the fragmentation of EU membership will eventually disappear as well.

But the closer we are to the present day, the harder it is to see clearly what constitutes which events are of major historical importance, and the easier it is to get lost in the minutiae of detail. Still, what we know is that the contemporary Scandinavian states are some of the happiest nations in the world, frequently topping rankings for gender equality, environmental sustainability, participatory democracy and more. To some extent, their success is a product of a long series of coincidences. Yet it has also been determined by the actions and decisions of Scandinavians themselves, always active agents in their own destiny.

Acknowledgments

I'd like to thank all the students who, over the last fifteen years, have taken part in my Scandinavian history and Nordic politics classes. Without you, I wouldn't have had the chance to think about the region's history in a more comprehensive and overarching way, as research usually leads one to focus on details and particularities. I'm also grateful to the institutions I've worked at during this time: the University of Tartu, in Estonia; University College London (UCL), in the United Kingdom; and Yale University, in the United States.

I would also like to thank my wonderful editors at Black Inc., who have been incredibly helpful and a pleasure to work with.

Further Reading

Arter, David, *Scandinavian Politics Today*, Manchester: Manchester University Press, 2016.

Gustafsson, Harald, *Nordens historia: En europeisk region under 1200 år*, Lund: Studentlitteratur, 2007.

Helle, Knut (ed.), *The Cambridge History of Scandinavia: Volume 1: Prehistory to 1520*, Cambridge: Cambridge University Press, 2003.

Hilson, Mary, *The Nordic Model: Scandinavia Since 1945*, London: Reaktion Books, 2008.

Kouri, Erkki Ilmari, and Jens E. Olesen (eds), *The Cambridge History of Scandinavia: Volume 2: 1520–1870*, Cambridge: Cambridge University Press, 2016.

Nedergaard, Peter, and Anders Wivel (eds), *The Routledge Handbook of Scandinavian Politics*, London: Routledge, 2017.

Nordstrom, Byron J., *Scandinavia Since 1500*, Minneapolis: University of Minnesota Press, 2000.

Østergaard, Uffe, "The Geopolitics of Nordic Identity: From Composite States to Nation States," in Bo Stråth and Øystein Sørensen (eds), *The Cultural Construction of Norden*, Oslo: Scandinavian University Press, 1997.

Salonen, Kirsi, and Kurt Villads Jensen, *Scandinavia in the Middle Ages 900–1550: Between Two Oceans*, London: Routledge, 2023

Sawyer, Birgit, and Peter Sawyer, *Medieval Scandinavia: From Conversion to Reformation, circa 800–1500*, Minneapolis: University of Minnesota Press, 1993.

Image Credits

Maps on pages 2, 21, 96, 183, 215 by Alan Laver

p. 9: Illustration by Marilyn de Castro. Adapted from an artwork by MuiDark. Image via Wikimedia Commons.

p. 12: Reproduced by permission of Gerhard Milstreu. Underslös Museum, Tanum World Heritage.

p. 38: Photograph by Casiopeia. Image via Wikimedia Commons.

p. 50: Unknown artist, fourteenth-century illustration. Image via Wikimedia Commons.

p. 60: Photograph by Jacob Truedson Demitz, assisted by Emil Eikner. Image via Southerly Clubs of Stockholm / Wikimedia Commons.

p. 67: Collection of Museum of Fine Arts, Leipzig. Image via Wikimedia Commons.

p. 72: David Frumerie [attributed to], after Jacob Binck, *Gustav I, 1497–1560, King of Sweden*, 1555. Collection of Stockholm National Museum. Image via Wikimedia Commons.

p. 75: Artwork by Sébastien Bourdon, 1653. Collection of Stockholm National Museum. Image via Wikimedia Commons.

p. 82: Artwork by David von Krafft, 1707. Collection of Stockholm National Museum. Image via Wikimedia Commons.

p. 88: Artwork by Hans Heysen, 1824, after Jens Juel, *Portrait of Johann Friedrich Struensee*, 1771. Collection of Rosenborg Castle, Copenhagen. Image via Wikimedia Commons.

p. 103: Artwork by Christoffer Wilhelm Eckersberg, 1807. Collection of The Museum of National History at Frederiksborg Castle, Denmark. Image via Wikimedia Commons.

p. 106: Artwork by Oscar Wergeland, 1885. Collection of Parliament of Norway Building. Image via Wikimedia Commons.

p. 109: Photograph by Daderot. Image via Wikimedia Commons.

p. 117: Artwork by Wilhelm Camphausens, 1864. Image via Wikimedia Commons.

p. 125: Unknown photographer. Collection of Stockholm City Museum. Image via Wikimedia Commons.

p. 127: Artwork by Johan Gustaf Sandberg, 1843. Collection of Gripsholm Castle. Image via Wikimedia Commons.

p. 132: Unknown manufacturer, commissioned by National Association against Emigration. Collection of Småland Museum. Image via Digital Museum.
p. 138: Photograph by Lars Larsson, c. 1900–07. Image via Wikimedia Commons.
p. 142: Photograph by Ernest Rude. Collection of the United States Library of Congress. Image via Wikimedia Commons.
p. 147: Unknown photographer, 1914. Image via Wikimedia Commons.
p. 150: TT News Agency / Alamy Stock Photo.
p. 158: Photograph by Gösta Florman. Collection of The Royal Library, Sweden. Image via Wikimedia Commons.
p. 161: Unknown photographer, 1928. Image via Kvsallsstuden.se.
p. 169: Artwork by Fritz Rückert, 1940.
p. 175: Photograph by Mogens Margolinsky, 1943. © Frihedsmuseet.
p. 182: Collection of Arbeiderbevegelsen's Archive and Library. CC BY-NC-ND.
p. 187: Photograph by Kalle Kultala, 1960. Image via Wikimedia Commons.
p. 191: Photograph by Holger Ellgaard, 1971. Image via Wikimedia Commons.
p. 202: Jens Glargård / Ritzau Scanpix.
p. 209: Photograph courtesy of World Economic Forum. Image via Wikimedia Commons.

Index

Note: Page numbers in bold refer to illustrations.

ABOUT THE AUTHOR

MART KULDKEPP is professor of Estonian and Nordic history at University College London. His special area of interest is the transnational connections between the Nordic and the Baltic countries, especially in the early 20th century.

martk.net | @kuldkeppmart